THE

ECONOMIC WRITINGS

OF

FRANCIS HORNER

IN THE

EDINBURGH REVIEW

1802–6

*Series of Reprints of Scarce Works on
Political Economy*

No. 13

THE

ECONOMIC WRITINGS

OF

FRANCIS HORNER

IN THE

EDINBURGH REVIEW

1802-6

Edited
With an Introduction by
FRANK WHITSON FETTER

THE LONDON SCHOOL
OF ECONOMICS AND POLITICAL SCIENCE
(*University of London*)
HOUGHTON STREET, ALDWYCH, LONDON, W.C.2
1957

Made in Great Britain at the Pitman Press, Bath

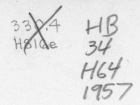
NOTE

There were many reprintings of early volumes of the *Edinburgh Review*. For the text here the following editions have been used:

Vol.	I—1802–3	10th Ed.—1814
	II—1803	7th Ed.—1814
	V—1804–5	6th Ed.—1815
	VII—1805–6	1st Ed.—1806

There are minor variations in spelling as between the different editions, but apparently the only two substantive changes were a footnote to the review of "Thornton's Paper Credit of Great Britain," that was added in the 4th edition, and the first sentence of the second paragraph of "The Utility of Country Banks Considered." These two changes are noted in the text where they occur. Except for one or two quite obvious mistakes the spelling and punctuation are reproduced exactly from the above editions.

CONTENTS

PAGE

INTRODUCTION: FRANCIS HORNER AND THE *EDINBURGH REVIEW*   1

Horner's Articles in *Edinburgh Review*, not here reprinted, and other Anonymous Publications.   20

Authority for Assignment of Authorship of *Edinburgh Review* Articles and other Publications to Francis Horner.   20

HORNER'S ECONOMIC ARTICLES IN THE *EDINBURGH REVIEW*   23

Irvine's Emigration from the Highlands.
Vol. I, No. I, October 1802, vii.   23

The Utility of Country Banks.
Vol. I, No. I, October 1802, xiv.   25

Thornton on the Paper Credit of Great Britain.
Vol. I, No. I, October 1802, xxv.   28

Canard's Principes d'Economie Politique.
Vol. I, No. II, January 1803, xvi.   57

Lord King's Thoughts on the Restriction of Payments in Specie at the Banks of England and Ireland.
Vol. II, No. IV, July 1803, xi.   77

Observations on the Bounty upon Exported Corn.
Vol. V, No. IX, October 1804, xv.   96

Lord Selkirk on Emigration.
Vol. VII, No. XIII, October 1805, xiii.   115

Playfair's Edition of Wealth of Nations.
Vol. VII, No. XIV, January 1806, xi.   133

INTRODUCTION

FRANCIS HORNER AND THE *EDINBURGH REVIEW*

The 'Edinburgh Review' as an Economic Journal

THE *Edinburgh Review*, established in 1802, was not thought of, either by its founders or by its readers, as an economic journal, but rather as a survey of the whole field of literature, public affairs, and human knowledge. However, the circumstances of the time, and the accidents of personality, soon made it, among other things, a powerful organ of economic opinion. Economic problems were forcing themselves on public attention, both in and out of Parliament, around the turn of the century. Monetary policy, the position of the Bank of England, population, the condition of the poor, and the corn laws as England shifted from an exporter to an importer of wheat, undoubtedly would have become important issues with a continuation of the gradual economic changes of the latter decades of the eighteenth century. These problems, however, were brought dramatically before the public by the developments of the Napoleonic wars and their immediate aftermath.

The *Edinburgh Review*, from its first issue, discussed economic problems, and until mid-century economic articles held a prominent place in its pages. The newer reviews, the *Quarterly Review*, established in 1809 as an answer to the increasingly Whig bias of the *Edinburgh*, *Blackwood's Edinburgh Magazine*, started in 1817, and the *Westminster Review*, founded in 1824, all published many economic articles, but none of these journals equalled the *Edinburgh* either in contemporary economic influence or in significance in the history of economic thought. For nearly fifty years the tone of the economic articles in the *Edinburgh Review* was set, in turn, by three men: Francis Horner, John Ramsay McCulloch, and Nassau Senior. McCulloch and Senior are well known to present-day economists: McCulloch primarily as an unoriginal, but highly effective, spokesman for free competition, and as a popularizer of Ricardian economics; Senior as an economic adviser of government, an original thinker in some aspects of foreign trade and interest theory, and the first professor of political economy at Oxford. Francis Horner's name is less known to economists, and in so far as he is included in the fraternity of economists it is usually as the prime mover and chairman of the Bullion Committee of 1810. His writing for the *Edinburgh Review* covered a shorter period, and he produced fewer articles than did his successors as the economists of the *Edinburgh*: eight economic articles, all in the years 1802–1806, and six on other subjects, by Horner; seventy-eight articles, all bearing on economics, by McCulloch in 1818–1837; and eleven economic articles by Senior in 1841–1849.

1

Horner's Influence on the Economic Articles in the 'Edinburgh Review'

Three of Horner's economic articles were little more than short descriptive notes. Of the five longer articles one dealt with Scottish emigration, but the other four longer articles represented substantial economic analysis. The significance of Horner's economic contributions to the *Edinburgh Review* is not to be measured, however, by the number of his articles. It was his influence, more than that of any other man, that caused the *Edinburgh*, from the first issue, to give economic problems a prominent place. The founders of the *Edinburgh Review* were all Whig in their sympathies, and within a few years, in part as a result of Henry Brougham's influence, it became increasingly an organ of Whig opinion in the political field. In the field of economics, however, its position, although favourable to the Whig view, rarely was a narrowly partisan one during Horner's life. Its political and economic approach was in the tradition of Adam Smith: a desire to shake off the dead hand of outmoded laws and regulations, an interest in human institutions as instruments to serve the welfare of man, a greater trust in the market than in the legislature to give the right solution, and an impatience with the more extreme forms of the aristocratic tradition.

Many references in contemporary books, pamphlets, and the press to the *Edinburgh Review*'s early articles on economic topics—most of them from Horner's pen—bespeak the influence that Horner had in presenting economic problems to the reading public in terms of reasoned analysis. A notable example is Ricardo's discussion in the chapter of his *Principles* on 'Bounties on Exportation, and Prohibitions of Importation,' where he quoted extensively from Horner's review of October 1804 on 'Observations on the Bounty upon Exported Corn,' and used it as a point of departure for his own analysis of how, in the Ricardian system, changes in the prices of food would affect profits rather than the prices of other commodities, as Horner had reasoned. Horner's influence seems to have been particularly great in the money and banking field, not only in helping to shape economic thinking in the early days of the Bank Restriction, but in stimulating others to examine further the problems of theory and policy raised by inconvertible paper money. Undoubtedly Ricardo had reference to some of Horner's articles when he wrote in 1818 in a reminiscent letter to his friend Hutches Trower:*

> I remember well the pleasure I felt, when I first discovered that you, as well as myself, was a great admirer of the work of Adam Smith, and of the early articles on Political Economy which had appeared in the Edinburgh Review. Meeting as we did every day, these afforded us often an agreeable subject for half an hour's chat, when business did not engage us.

* *The Works and Correspondence of David Ricardo.* Edited by Piero Sraffa with the collaboration of M. H. Dobb. 10 vol. Cambridge, 1951–1955. vol. vii, p. 246.

Nicholas Vansittart, Joint Secretary of the Treasury, who later in 1811 was a leading Parliamentary critic of the Bullion Report, and of the ideas associated with Ricardo of the influence of monetary action on prices and the foreign exchanges, apparently also was reading with appreciation Horner's early articles. Henry Brougham, in an unpublished letter to Horner in December 1803, said:*

> I rejoice to hear that Vansittart asked to be made acquainted with you—for I understand that he is a reading man and conclude that his desires were excited by reading your articles.

J. C. Herries, the Commissary General of the Army, and a severe critic of the Bullion Report, in an anonymous pamphlet of 1811 referred to the *Edinburgh Review* as 'the parent, nurse, and champion of the Bullion Committee.'† This was misleading in the suggestion that the *Edinburgh Review* had carried on a campaign either to have the Bullion Committee appointed, or to support its recommendations. Herries was correct, however, in the larger sense that the articles in the *Edinburgh Review* had been a powerful stimulus in arousing public interest, from 1802 on, in the issues of monetary and banking policy, and preparing the way for the full-scale debate of 1810 and 1811.

Horner's Early Life and Education

Francis Horner was born in Edinburgh on August 12, 1778, the eldest son of a Scottish merchant. His early education was in Edinburgh, and in 1792, at the age of fourteen—the same age at which Adam Smith went to the University of Glasgow—he entered the University of Edinburgh. At that time the Scottish universities, and particularly Edinburgh, were centres of pioneering thought and intellectual ferment, both among faculty and students. Horner attended the lectures of some of the great teachers of the day, and was active in the student literary society.

Horner planned to enter the law, and after three years at the University of Edinburgh, his father arranged for him to live for a year with the Rev. John Hewlett, who had a school in Shacklewell, Middlesex. As his brother, Leonard Horner, expressed it in the *Memoirs of Francis Horner*:‡

> He had as yet lived constantly at home; but his father being anxious to give him those advantages which a youth derives from being thrown upon his own resources among strangers, and at the same time, thinking it desirable that he should be freed from the disadvantages of a provincial dialect to a public speaker, it was determined that, for the next year at least, he should prosecute his studies in England.

* All quotations from letters to and from Horner, for which no citation is given, are from the unpublished Horner papers at the London School of Economics.
† *A Review of the Controversy Respecting the High Price of Bullion and the State of Our Currency*, pp. 5–6.
‡ Vol. i, p. 5.

3

The arrangement proved so satisfactory that the stay was extended to two years. Both a contemporary letter of Hewlett's, and testimony of others, indicate that the stay in England was successful in giving Horner a speech that revealed little evidence of early life north of the border; and his own letters show mature thought on economic problems and public affairs. Two passages in these letters are of particular interest in view of Horner's later writings on monetary problems, and his political career. On March 17, 1797, less than three weeks after the Bank Restriction, he wrote to his father:*

> Paper money still circulates without depreciation, and must be found, in the mean time, a great relief to the market; for many reasons, especially the enlargement of the Bank discounts. All political reasonings point out the increase of paper currency as a most pernicious evil; but it is to be hoped, that matters may yet go on well, provided it be used only as a temporary expedient.

In the same letter, after a discussion of the political situation, and his hopes for a career in law and public life, he said:†

> . . . I often look forward to a rule of conduct, which I hope no circumstances may ever induce me to abandon; and it is this, to connect myself with the exclusive interests of no political party whatever. A man's independence must be best preserved, and his duty to the public best performed, by attaching himself, not to any set of political characters, but to that system of measures which he believes most conducive to the public welfare. It seems a reasonable duty, at all times, rather to lean towards the ruling ministers; for no administration can act with the energy that it ought, unless it can trust to the countenance of respectable people.

One of Horner's activities, while living with Hewlett, is evidence of his intellectual qualities and his breadth of interests at this time. Under the supervision of Hewlett, he translated from the French edition—the original had been in German—*Elements of Algebra* by Leonhard Euler, whose name is today familiar to economists through Euler's theorem. This first English translation of Euler, with a biographical sketch that Horner wrote, was published in two volumes in 1797, and this translation went through five editions, the latest in 1840.

On his return to Edinburgh, Horner spent the next five years in study for the bar and in starting the practice of law.‡ At the same time he attended lectures at the University, including those on political economy by Dugald Stewart, the student and biographer of Adam Smith, and continued an ambitious reading programme. As was true of many young men of the day, he read extensively in Gibbon, and he

---

* *Memoirs*, vol. i, pp. 34–35.
† *Ibid*, pp. 35–36.
‡ A large part of vol. i, pp. 57–217, of the *Memoirs* consists of the journal that Horner kept between his return to Edinburgh in 1797 and his move to London in 1803.

4

seems to have made a conscious effort to cultivate a Gibbonesque style, which was later reflected in the phrasing of some of his *Edinburgh* reviews. His reading, and his activities in the local Philosophical Society, show evidence of an increasing interest in economic problems: reading of Turgot, whose economic works he talked of translating for publication, and of other French 'economists'; study of Adam Smith, and many comments on the *Wealth of Nations*; and reading and thinking on the population problem, on which he wrote an essay for the Academy of Physics. He started a paper for the Speculative Society on 'The Circulation of Money,' and his sage comment, when barely twenty-one, 'I find the circulation of money a very dark subject, though a few gleams of light have struck me,' has been re-echoed by many older economists. Four days before the paper was to be given, he reported in his journal that he found it 'a subject of too great difficulty' and had given it up. He then prepared for the Society a paper on 'the influence of the great commercial metropolis on the prosperity of the state,' which he reported was not difficult as he 'had often made this a topic of reflection.'

A letter written to the Duke of Somerset in January 1802, at the suggestion of the Duke's brother, giving a list of economic works and commenting on their contents, showed a familiarity with economic literature, both English and French, that few men of his day, no matter what their age, could have equalled. Horner's closing comment was much more than the ostentation of callow youth:

> If there is any particular brand of Political Economy to which your grace proposed to direct your attention, it will give me real and very flattering pleasure to aid you in completing the list of books to be consulted.

A few months later, when his friend John Allen went to the Continent with Lord Holland, after the Peace of Amiens, Horner prepared twenty-eight queries in regard to economic and political problems on which he asked Allen to look for information. These showed a remarkable grasp of the important economic issues, covering such topics as the fields into which investment was flowing, the rate of interest, the use that 'the *nouveaux riches*, who have amassed fortunes by contracts &c. during the war', have made of their funds, the condition of agriculture, the developments in manufacturing, arrangements for 'the maintenance of the destitute poor,' population changes, and the general query:

> Is there any class of literati, who attach themselves to political economy? If there be, what are their leading doctrines, particularly with regard to the theory of national wealth, the freedom of industry, and legislative interference?
>
> Is the peculiar system of the Economists forgotten, or does it still preserve some advocates?
>
> In what estimation is the character of Turgot, &c. held?

In so far as it is true that one of the tests of a good economist is to know what questions to ask, Horner ranked high even at the age of twenty-three.

His letter to Allen also made extensive requests for the purchase of books in economics. Letters to other friends over many years show the same avidity for economic literature, and also indicate that he read extensively in the books that he acquired. There is no way of knowing whether Horner's library, sold at auction in 1831, contained all of his books, but what was sold that year was a comprehensive collection, including much French and some Spanish material, and a wealth of British material, both contemporary and earlier eighteenth century.*

Although Horner's interest in economics started at a younger age than did Ricardo's and—at least up to around 1810—led to much more reading, they had two things in common: Adam Smith was for both their first extended reading in economics; and they shared an early interest in the natural sciences, including chemistry. An example of Horner's broad approach to economics is an entry in his journal in 1800, after references to chemistry, geology, and the manufacture of tobacco pipes:

> A knowledge of the arts, as they are practised in different parts of the country, is what I am desirous to possess on many accounts; but especially the subserviency of such knowledge to the study of political economy.

Founding of the 'Edinburgh Review' and Horner's Articles

In the spring of 1802 Horner was one of a group of young Scots, who with Sydney Smith, an English clergyman without a living then in Edinburgh as tutor to an English boy, planned the *Edinburgh Review*. The first issue appeared in October 1802, and of the twenty-nine articles Horner contributed four, of which three were on economic topics, including a review of Henry Thornton's *An Enquiry into the Nature and Effects of the Paper Credit of Great Britain*, that had been published early in 1802.

Thornton's book, like practically all of the monetary and banking literature of the period, had been inspired by the issues arising out of the suspension of cash payments by the Bank of England in February 1797. But it was a very different sort of work, both in its spirit and its coverage, from other contemporary publications. Thornton was a successful banker, a member of Parliament since 1782, and a prominent lay religious figure and a leader in the Clapham Sect, whose members, including Wilberforce and Zachary Macaulay, the father of Thomas Babington Macaulay, played so active a role in stimulating the conscience of England on slavery, on education, and on 'good works' in general. Most of the previous publications on the Bank Restriction had been biased either by political considerations or economic interest, had attempted to prove a point rather than to analyse a situation,

* The sale was made by Mr. R. H. Evans at 93, Pall Mall on March 30, 1831. A printed catalog of the collection, with marginal notes giving the purchaser and the price at which each item was sold, is in the New York Public Library.

and were often written with little attention to the practices of the money market or the foreign exchanges. Thornton brought to bear on the problem a judicious approach, and a thorough familiarity with the details of banking practice. He had been a witness before the Lords and Commons committees of 1797 that investigated the suspension of cash payments, and the book incorporated many of the ideas that he had developed at that time. The result was a classic, that with the exception of Malthus' *Essay on the Principle of Population* was the outstanding English economic work between Smith's *Wealth of Nations* and Ricardo's *Principles of Political Economy*. But Thornton's long discussions of banking practice, and of the relations between country banks, London banks, and the Bank of England, were not ones to hold the ordinary reader's attention, and often obscured the main points in the exposition of the relation of monetary expansion, and of foreign payments, to the foreign exchanges. In some passages Thornton did not differentiate clearly between the mechanism of adjustment under convertible and inconvertible currency. Horner's review summarized the main points in Thornton's analysis, freed from the mass of detail, and also made clear the difference in adjustment under convertible and inconvertible conditions. Horner gave a reasoned defence of convertibility as a monetary objective, while at the same time recognizing that this might not be practical in a war situation. The review was both an exposition that carried the message of Thornton's book to a much wider audience than the readers of the book, and a positive contribution to economic analysis.

The first issue of the *Edinburgh Review* had a success that surpassed the greatest hopes of its founders. Horner's interest in the *Edinburgh*, and his desire to contribute, continued, but his ambitions for writing outran his achievements. The versatility of his interests, combined with procrastination and a love of perfection, meant that over the next ten years the books that he talked of reviewing far outnumbered those that he reviewed. Sydney Smith wrote from London to Francis Jeffrey, the editor, in November 1803, in regard to the selection of books to be reviewed by the *Edinburgh*:*

> I will stop such books as I want myself; but you had better give Horner a caution against stopping more books than he wants, as he is a sort of literary tiger, whose den is strewed with ten times more victims than he can devour.

Undoubtedly a contributing factor in Horner's failure to realize his ambitions as a reviewer was his decision, in 1802, to follow the path that so many ambitious Scots have taken, before and since, and seek his fortune in London. In March of 1802, he visited London, primarily to consider whether to join the English bar, and decided to do so. However, it was not until March 1803 that he made the move to London. Before he went to London he wrote for the second issue a

* *The Letters of Sydney Smith.* Edited by Nowell C. Smith. 2 vol., Oxford, 1953. vol. i, p. 91.

long and critical review of Canard's *Principes d'Economie Politique*, a mediocre work that acquired an undeserved fame from having been awarded a prize by the National Institute of France. Canard had made extensive use of mathematical symbols, and Horner's discussion of the usefulness and the limitations of mathematics in economics has a modern ring to it, and is of particular interest in the light of his own work on Euler's *Algebra*:

In its own province, the peculiar language of algebra will never fail to gratify those who can appreciate the admirable structure of the most perfect instrument that has yet been invented by man. But that injudicious and unskilful pedantry ought most severely to be censured, which diverts an instrument from its proper use, and attempts to remove those landmarks by which the sciences are bounded from each other. The peculiar forms of expression, which have been introduced into the modern analysis, are sanctioned by the facilities which they afford, both of perspicuous abridgement, and of prosecuting a train of investigation to new and remote results. But M. Canard has only translated, into a language less readily understood, truths, of which the ordinary enunciation is intelligible and familiar to all. We will not deny that some branches of political economy, especially those which relate to circulation, money, and the analysis of price, admit of being treated with a precision which almost approaches to mathematical exactness. But a subject may possess this precision, without requiring, or even admitting, the symbolic representations of algebra.

After Horner's move to London the history of his reviewing was that of a constant internal struggle to reconcile his desire to be interested in the whole field of knowledge, to do more things than any man could reasonably accomplish, and at the same time to hold himself to a high standard of perfection. The first of Horner's articles written from London was the review, in July 1803, of Lord King's *Thoughts on the Restriction of Payments in Specie at the Banks of England and Ireland*. This influential work had been inspired by the depreciation, of nearly ten per cent, of the Irish pound in terms of the Bank of England note early in 1803, and was the expansion of a speech that King had given in the House of Lords in May 1803 on the condition of the Irish currency. Horner applied in the new setting of further depreciation the same discriminating exposition and analysis as in the Thornton review, and brought from Henry Brougham the praise:

. . . I think it not only by far the best of No. IV—that is small praise—I even think it better than your own former articles—Thornton and Canard.

In this review, Horner showed a greater concern about the dangers of inconvertible paper money than in his review of Thornton. Against the background of the depreciation of the Irish currency he had already moved far toward the doctrine of the Bullion Report, that convertibility was a necessary basis for a sound monetary system.

The article 'Observations on the Bounty upon Exported Corn' in October 1804, referred to earlier, was an analysis of the theoretical issues involved in a production bounty and an export bounty. Horner's review in October 1805 of 'Lord Selkirk on Emigration' had little of the theoretical analysis that had marked the four previous major reviews. It was rather as a Scot than as an economist that he wrote in this case. Yet he showed economic insight, free from the sentimentality that marked so much writing about the Highlands, in his recognition that the opening up of new opportunities elsewhere created an urge to migrate that the Government should not oppose. What Horner wrote then might well be applied to similar situations today:

> Considering the book in this aspect, it appears to us to possess a permanent value, beyond the effect it is calculated to produce in enlightening our own Government respecting the nature of this actual crisis. Other parts of our own empire yet remain to undergo a similar change; and other countries in the world, at least, all other countries that are destined to improve, and that include a sufficient extent of territory for the various branches of productive economy. Wherever cultivation may be heightened by the investing of new capital, the minute subdivision of land will be swept away for farmers of a different race; and wherever the extended territory of a thriving nation is diversified by a range of mountains, these will at length be appropriated to pasture walks. The particulars, therefore, which Lord Selkirk has related in the history of the Highlands, may be regarded as the description of a general change; for which, in all such countries, legislators ought to be prepared, that they may not, like our English statesmen of old, even Sir Thomas More and Lord Bacon, mistake, as symptoms of decay and devastation, the movements actually occasioned by the growth of wealth, enterprize, and industry.

Horner's final economic contribution was the shortest of all, a bare page of critical comment on the recent Playfair edition of the *Wealth of Nations*. He wrote, when he sent it to Jeffrey:

> I have written out my oracle on Playfair's W. of N. I only wish to stop its sale, and should have taken no notice of it but for this purpose—to inflict a merited punishment on the cupidity of booksellers.

Friendship of Horner and Malthus

The story of Horner's never completed review of Malthus' *Essay on the Principle of Population* is important not only as a symbol of the gap between Horner's intentions and his achievements as a reviewer, but because of its relation to the friendship of Horner and Malthus, and probably indirectly to the historic friendship and correspondence of Ricardo and Malthus. Early in 1799 Horner was writing an 'essay on *Population*' for the Academy of Physics in Edinburgh. In 1803 he was planning a review of the second edition of Malthus' *Essay* for the *Edinburgh*, and for several years the proposed review of Malthus was

9

a continual source of jesting and chiding in letters to and from Horner, and from others to Jeffrey. A footnote in the issue of October 1804, in his 'Observation on the Bounty upon Exported Corn,' spoke of such a review as appearing in an early issue. It never did, but Horner's interest in Malthus' work was the occasion for their meeting, and probably for the enlisting of Malthus as a contributor to the *Edinburgh Review*.

In January 1804 Horner had written to Jeffrey:

> In about a week hence I mean to set about Malthus for you, and mean to work at it very seriously; his book has made itself a great name among the thinking people here. That I may judge it with more freedom, I have declined one or two opportunities of cultivating the author's acquaintance; which I mean however to do, when I get loose from my task. He is a man in conversation of good sense, great candour, and liberality; the last is a rare qualification for an English clergyman, even after the splendid instance of our friend [Sydney] Smith.

In July 1807 Horner wrote to Lord Webb Seymour, a friend from Edinburgh days:*

> . . . Malthus has been a day or two in town; and gave me a little of his society, enough to enable me to judge of him; and I am happy to say, that a more philosophic candour, calm love of truth, and ingenious turn for speculation in his important branch, I have seldom met with.

Horner visited Malthus at Haileybury not later than 1808, and from then until 1815 there are many references to meetings in London, Horner's visits with Malthus at Haileybury, and exchanges of letters that show a friendship marked by mutual respect and the seeking of each other's opinions. In February 1808, shortly after Malthus' first article—'Spence on Commerce'—had appeared in the *Edinburgh*, Horner wrote to Jeffrey:†

> Since Malthus has begun to contribute, I hope it will not be for want of solicitation on your part, if he does not continue to supply you with articles. Of all subjects, political economy is at present the most productive of useful publications, and though his general views are sometimes imperfect, he is always candid, and an advocate of what he believes to be most liberal and generous.

Horner was directly responsible for Malthus' two contributions on the Bullion Controversy to the *Edinburgh Review* in February and August 1811. Horner had originally intended to write something for the *Edinburgh Review* on the monetary situation, following the presentation of the Bullion Report, but abandoned the idea and finally turned to Malthus after he was unable to persuade Ricardo to write for the *Edinburgh Review*.‡

---

* *Memoirs*, vol. i, p. 433.   † *Memoirs*, vol. i, p. 446.

‡ Details on the negotiations that led up to Malthus' contribution are given by Piero Sraffa, in the Ricardo *Works*, vol. iii, pp. 9–12, and in my 'The Authorship of Economic Articles in the *Edinburgh Review*, 1802–47,' *The Journal of Political Economy*, vol. lxi, June 1953, pp. 236–237.

Malthus' contribution on the Bullion Controversy is the most notable, and the best documented, case of Horner's influence on the economic content of the *Edinburgh Review* even after he had ceased to write for it. But from the founding of the *Review* almost to the time of his death, Horner was calling Jeffrey's attention to books for review, outlining to him a broad economic philosophy that transcended party politics, suggesting reviewers, urging on old reviewers that they do further writing and even suggesting the general approach they might take. In at least one instance, in the role of London literary agent for the *Edinburgh*, he made additions to a manuscript before sending it on to Jeffrey. That Horner, as late as 1814, still played with the idea of again writing for the *Edinburgh*, is indicated by a letter from Jeffrey to Malthus, congratulating Malthus on his recent pamphlets on the corn trade. He chided Malthus for not having put the material into a review, and added:*

I trust, however, that you will not spoil me a review as well as tantalize me by having missed one so excellent. Horner had promised to give me some remarks on the subject, but I am half afraid your pamphlet will put him in despair.

In the latter part of 1816 Horner, who for some months had been suffering from a congestion of the lungs, left, with his brother Leonard, for the warmer climate of Italy in the hope of recovering his health. His condition became worse, and he died in Pisa on February 8, 1817 and was buried in the Protestant cemetery in Leghorn. A monument to him is in Westminster Abbey.

Professional and Organizational Activities

Horner's connection with the *Edinburgh Review* was only a small part of a full life. From December 1806 until his death he was, except for a few months, a member of Parliament. In addition to the ordinary run of legal work, early in 1806, on the nomination of Lord Minto, he was appointed to the Carnatic Commission—a Board of Commissioners established by the East India Company—for settling the disputed claims of the creditors of the Nabob of Arcot. This position was not a sinecure, and after three years he resigned on account of the pressure of other activities. A letter from Sydney Smith to Francis Jeffrey in February 1808 is evidence on the wide interests of Horner.†

Of our friend Horner I do not see much. He has four distinct occupations, each of which may very fairly occupy the life of a man not deficient in activity: the Carnatic Commission, the Chancery Bar, Parliament, and a very numerous and select acquaintance.

He joined, when he first visited London in 1802, The King of Clubs, a club that Ricardo and Malthus later joined, and that is frequently

---

* Lord Cockburn: *Life of Lord Jeffrey with a Selection from His Correspondence.* 2 vol. Edinburgh, 1852. vol. ii, p. 145.
† *The Letters of Sydney Smith.* vol. i, p. 133.

mentioned in the Ricardo-Malthus correspondence. In 1807 he became a member of Brooks', a famous club whose members were mostly of Whig sympathies, and that Ricardo joined in 1818. He belonged to the Geological Society of London, as did Ricardo, and by a coincidence, while the Bullion Committee was in session in April 1810, he and Ricardo were elected to the seven-man board of permanent trustees, and served together until Horner's death. He was a member of the African Institution, an organization interested in suppressing the slave trade and in general improving the position of the Negro. The driving force in the Institution were the 'Saints' of the Clapham Sect. Although Horner was not a member of the Clapham Sect, his views on slavery and on education were in line with their views. In and out of Parliament his influence was in support of the Clapham Sect on their main political and educational objectives, and in 1815 he prepared a *Special Report of The Directors of The African Institution*, defending the Institution against recent charges that had been brought against it.

The Economist in Parliament

The idea of political life had appealed to Horner even as a boy, and it is probable that his move to London in 1803 was influenced by political ambitions. He entered Parliament in 1806 by almost the only way that, in the unreformed Parliament of the day, one not of the landed gentry or a son of the nobility, or not prepared to purchase a seat from a borough monger, could hope to do so: by the patronage of a borough owner. Lord Kinnaird offered Horner a seat for St. Ives; Horner accepted, was elected in November 1806, and took his seat the following month. He was not returned in the elections in May 1807, but in July of that year was chosen in a by-election for Wendover, through the influence of Lord Carrington. This seat he gave up in 1812, and his frank statement in an unfinished letter to Sydney Smith is a vignette on election practices in the time of the unreformed Parliament.*

> As to Parliament, I have no seat, because Lord Carrington, to whom I owed my last, has to provide for a nephew, who has come of age since the last election, as well as for his son-in-law . . .; and because I have not money, or popularity of my own, to obtain a seat in the more regular and desirable way.

He was not out of Parliament for long, for in March 1813 he was offered a seat for St. Mawes by the Marquis of Buckingham, entered Parliament the following month, and held the seat until his death. The letter from Horner's friend William Freemantle, writing on behalf of the Marquis of Buckingham, is further commentary on contemporary politics:†

> I have reason to know that a seat will be vacant in the course of

* *Memoirs*, vol. ii, pp. 115–116.
† *Ibid.*, p. 130.

12

ten days, which I am authorized to offer you, begging you to understand it to be without stipulation or pledge of any sort or kind, saving that which, of course, you would feel it just to admit, namely, to resign whenever your politics should differ from the person who has the means of recommending you to the seat. The expense will be merely the dinner, which I rather think does not usually amount to more than 30*l*. or 40*l*.

Horner always held his Parliamentary seat by the support of a Whig patron. But he was not a hidebound party man, and both in his association with the *Edinburgh Review* and in Parliament his weight was always thrown against narrow partisanship. He had a sympathy with reform movements in all fields, but without the zealot's fire, for he frequently had doubts as to the correctness of his own views, and he was unwilling to support, in the interests of party unity, a position in which he did not believe. This devotion to principle is shown by an incident in 1811, when Lord Grenville asked Horner to be a Secretary of the Treasury in case a new Government were formed with Grenville as head of the Treasury. The talked-of Government was never formed, but even had it been Horner would not have been a member, for he rejected Lord Grenville's proposal. As he wrote to his friend, John Archibald Murray, later a judge of the Scottish court of session:*

> . . . I have been put to the trial, and have decided without any difficulty to adhere to the rule which I laid down for myself when I went into Parliament, not to take any political office until I was rich enough to live at ease out of office.

Horner's leadership in bringing the currency question before Parliament in 1810, which led to the Report of the Bullion Committee, of which he was a co-author, and to the debate on that Report, was his most famous Parliamentary action. This, however, was only one aspect of ten years of Parliamentary activity in which he was a vigorous spokesman for correction of the abuses of the judicial system, softening of the severities of the penal code, elimination of sinecures of church and state, greater educational opportunities, removal of the disabilities on Catholics, more equitable treatment for Ireland, a defence of the rights of Scotland and of the Church of Scotland, and elimination of the slave trade. Horner was a supporter of the market, and of non-interference of government, as a means of getting rid of the abuses of privilege and of encouraging the better utilization of the nation's productive powers. His faith in political economy was, however, always tempered by a belief in a national interest that might transcend the immediate economic gain, and that made his devotion to 'economic laws' less dedicated than that of Ricardo, of McCulloch, or of Cobden and Bright. A passage in his *Edinburgh Review* article, 'Observations on the Bounty upon Exported Corn', is a good summary of Horner's economic philosophy:

* *Memoirs*, vol. ii, p. 55.

13

If that sort of encouragement to tillage, which we have here admitted, should be deemed a sufficient benefit to recommend to a great nation the establishment of a bounty, it must still be remembered that, though it may indirectly secure a more certain supply of corn, it necessarily retards, upon the whole, the growth of national opulence and industry. It forces a part of the national capital into a branch of trade, which is necessarily a losing one, and which does not return the whole of the capital that is employed in it. Defence, however, it has been said, is of more importance than opulence:* and an independent supply of subsistence lies at the foundation of the means of defence. The general observation is undeniable. The truths of political economy form but a class among the principles of administration, and in their practical application must often be limited by higher maxims of state, to which in theory too they are held subordinate, as being less general. Yet, unless this subordination is finely and truly felt, the limit may be placed very injudiciously; and we may be summoned to deviate from general rules, whenever a statesman takes fright at a temporary inconvenience, or is captivated with some specious project of a remedy.

Horner's Parliamentary interests were broader than were Ricardo's, but he came closer than anyone before Ricardo to being the political economist in Parliament. James Mill, who in 1814 and 1815 had suggested to Ricardo that he seek a seat in Parliament, took the occasion in 1816 of Horner's absence from Parliament in Italy again to urge the matter on Ricardo:†

He will be a very great loss—even his absence this winter is grievously to be deplored—when so many foolish, and I fear, some villainous schemes of finance, will be proposed and listened to. You ought indeed to be in parliament, . . .

Ricardo's reply showed his respect for Horner, and suggests the tempered quality of Horner's approach to public issues:‡

The absence of Horner is indeed a great loss. I meet with no one who does not lament his illness. Whatever he has undertaken he has done well, and has always avoided the error into which I think Brougham is apt to fall, he never goes beyond the mark, he never endeavors to prove too much.

Even though Ricardo and Horner, in the particular setting of the times, were both critics of the Bank of England, there was, aside from the theoretical issue of the relative importance of monetary and non-monetary influences on exchange rates, a subtle but nevertheless real difference in social philosophy. Whereas Ricardo's stress was more on the abuses of a monopoly, Horner's was more on the failure of the

* Wealth of Nations, II, 195. [Horner's footnote.]
† Ricardo, *Works*, vol. vii, p. 85.
‡ *Ibid.*, pp. 89–90.

14

Bank directors to have a broader economic understanding or social vision. Horner's view on Bank of England policy seems to have been part of a general philosophy that there sometimes were, in issues of economic policy, considerations of public policy that overrode any analysis of the market. In December 1810, between the publication of the Bullion Report and the Parliamentary debate on it, Horner wrote to John Archibald Murray:

> It is material, in my view of this [Bullion] question, to impress the public with the notion that it is a state question, not one of trade, to be decided by political considerations not by the notions of the counting house.

In the same spirit, he said in Parliament a few months later, in regard to the appointment of a committee on commercial credit, that 'he could not avoid thinking that it would have been better had it contained fewer commercial members.'*

This conflict and compromise between Horner's belief in 'economic laws', and his unwillingness to push that belief to the hilt, is illustrated by his position in 1808, on a bill that had been 'proposed with the consent of the masters as well as of the journeymen, to limit the excessive depreciation of the Wages of persons employed in the weaving of Cotton.' Following a speech by Davies Giddy opposing the bill, Hansard reported:†

> Mr. Horner agreed with almost every thing which had been said by the hon. gent. who had just sat down. But, however strong his conviction was of the impropriety of the principle on which this measure was to be founded, he thought the application of such a numerous and deserving class of individuals merited every attention; and perhaps in discussing the remedy which had been proposed by the right hon. gent. one less objectionable might be discovered.

Seven years later, when Sir Robert Peel brought in a bill to regulate the employment of apprentices in cotton mills, the Hansard account reads:‡

> Mr. Horner observed, that the former measures, and even the present Bill as far as he could understand its object, fell far short of what Parliament should do on the subject,

and Horner then cited some shocking abuses in the existing practice of apprenticing children.

He opposed, in 1809, a bounty on the production of Irish flax-seed.§ In 1813, 1814 and 1815 he opposed the new Corn Laws, and when in

* Hansard, vol. xix, 125.
† Vol. xi, 426.
‡ Vol. xxxi, 625.
§ Vol. xiii, 766.

the debate in February 1815 Sir John Newport made critical comments on political economists, Horner replied:*

> But as to political economy generally, upon what ground could gentlemen pretend to depreciate its character, unless they meant to deprecate the exercise of reasoning upon the subject under the consideration of the committee?

Yet in another debate, in 1814, on the Corn Laws:†

> He was aware that commerce should always give way to higher reasons of state: but it appeared to him that there was here no reason; . . .

In the discussion of the Bank Restriction in 1816, Horner was in the minority that wished the Bank to prepare for early resumption. In the debates in May 1816, his three motions for a select committee 'to inquire into the expediency of restoring the Cash Payments of the Bank of England, and the safest and most advantageous means of effecting it'; for the resumption of cash payments in two years; and for giving instructions that the Bank Directors take the necessary steps to prepare for resumption, were all defeated by large majorities.‡
In the light of modern economic analysis Horner's position on the resumption of payments in 1816, as in the Bullion controversy in 1810 and 1811, is subject to criticism in that it gave almost no attention to the problems of unemployment associated with deflation. His emphasis in 1816 seemed to be on the legal commitments that had been made: the Bank was pledged to resume, and he expected it to carry out its pledges. But it would be easy for a present-day critic to overstress the limitations of Horner's economic views on resumption. The Bank and its Parliamentary defenders had no clear-cut philosophy of a managed currency, or of the dangers of deflation, to put up against Horner's views, tainted though these may have been by legalism. Not only were both the Bank and the Government opposing any move for a definite resumption date, but they came dangerously close to the view that the operations of a Central Bank, including its dealings with Government, were purely private business operations, into which the public at large had no right to pry; and that there was no monetary philosophy by which the Bank of England should be guided in its credit operations beyond that of lending only on sound assets. It is reasonable to interpret Horner's position in 1816, not as primarily that the Bank must resume, come what may, but that the operations of the Bank, and the philosophy of its foreign exchange operations and of its loan policy, were not just private business details, but matters of great public importance on which the public were entitled to be fully informed. The position of the Bank and of the Government

* Vol. xxix, 1032.
† Vol. xxvii, 918.
‡ Vol. xxxiv, 166, 250, 407.

16

that they were opposed to a firm commitment to resume in 1818 was a defensible one, but their position that they were against any thorough examination of the Bank's operations, or any full-scale review of their views on monetary policy, was a quite different matter. So many issues of policy and personality were involved, and there was such an extensive background to the 1816 debate on monetary policy, that it is difficult to say if the real issue in 1816 was that of resumption, regardless of prices and employment, or the question whether the Bank's operations and monetary philosophy were private business matters or matters of public concern.

Criticism of British Foreign Policy

Horner was also active in the debate on foreign policy in 1814 to 1816. Up to Napoleon's abdication in 1814 he had supported the wars against France, although always with more emphasis on the need to have a responsible government in France and less on victory for its own sake, or for the sake of British national power, than was true with most of the Tory leaders. In the Peninsular campaign he had been particularly concerned about bringing into the struggle the democratic forces in Spain and in keeping faith with them.

After Napoleon's retirement to Elba in 1814 Horner became very critical of British foreign policy, in particular on the ground that the British Government had allowed Genoa to be transferred to Sardinia, in violation, as he believed, of the pledges given by the British Government; and had assisted in restoring a 'usurper' to the throne of Spain.*

After Napoleon's return from Elba, Horner opposed resuming hostilities against France before Napoleon had committed an act of aggression. Horner's view on foreign policy between Elba and Waterloo was one with which British historians have been but little more sympathetic than were Horner's contemporaries. It was grounded, however, on his firm belief that England should not attempt to force upon France the government of the Bourbons, and was taken only after a careful weighing of the dangers and the advantages of immediate action against Napoleon. He wrote to John Archibald Murray in April 1815:†

> So many persons, in whose judgment and public spirit I have the best confidence, are for hurrying into immediate war, that I am afraid almost to inquire about your sentiments on that point, lest I should find them differing from my own. . . . Not that I place much faith in these professions [of Napoleon], for in forming a practical decision as to what is best to be done, I would look upon them as entitled to none at all; although I think it not impossible that reflections in exile, and older years, may have given prudence some ascendancy in his plans, and not wholly out of his character

* Hansard, vol. xxix, 950–952, February 21, 1815; 1158–1160, March 1, 1815.
† Memoirs, vol. ii, pp. 245–246.

that he should set his ambitions as it were upon a new theory of greatness for its gratification. But in making the practical determination, what I would be guided by is this, that if we are to open a new Iliad of war against the military power of France, it is of the last importance that we should so commence it, as to stamp upon it, in the opinion of the people of the continent, its true character as a war of defence merely against aggrandizement. By going to war now, we go to war for the Bourbons, to force that feeble worn-out race upon the French; we go to war too, upon a still more hopeless, and in my sentiments unjustifiable principle, that of proscribing an individual, and through him the nation which has adopted him, as incapable of peace or truce.

Horner's disagreement with many of the Whig leaders, including the Marquis of Buckingham, to whom he owed his seat, led Horner to offer, in April 1815, to resign his seat. The Marquis preferred not to accept Horner's resignation unless the Parliamentary differences became more acute, which they did not, and Horner continued to hold the seat until his death.

After Waterloo, Horner continued his criticism of British foreign policy. His speech of February 20, 1816,* attacking the Treaties of Peace, was a masterful presentation of the case against the forcing upon France of a government repugnant to her people. His discriminating picture of the good features of the French Revolution, as distinguished from its abuses, and his sympathetic presentation of the need for public support to give stability to government, showed a broad historical view, keen social insight, and high political courage in supporting an unpopular position.

Contribution to the Development of Economics

Horner's relatively brief career in economic writing has won him no outstanding place in the history of economics, nor is any particular theoretical idea associated with his name. It is for the Bullion Report of 1810 that economists generally remember him, and even there he is all too frequently thought of as a spokesman for Ricardo. The fact is that Horner's writings on monetary matters were already widely read when Ricardo's interest in economics had scarcely expanded beyond the details of the Stock Exchange, and Horner's writings were one of the influences that directed Ricardo's fertile mind toward a systematic analysis of economic problems. Furthermore, in the specific issue of 1809–1811 over the causes of the exchange rate depreciation, there was a sharp difference between Horner's view that monetary policy was only one, albeit the most important in the setting of the time, of several influences acting on exchange rates, and Ricardo's view that monetary policy was the sole cause.

* Hansard, vol. xxxii, 770–792.

Horner's great contribution to economics was not a particular idea, so much as an attitude: that economic problems were important, and that they should be discussed in the light of an analysis of the facts, against the background of history, including the experience of other countries, rather than in a spirit of political partisanship. It was not primarily a systematic body of theory that Horner presented, but an orderly exposition of a problem, that gave to the reader the feeling that economic problems were fit topics for the educated man to discuss in the light of reasoned analysis.

In appraising the influence of Horner's articles, one should keep in mind the large audience reached by the *Edinburgh Review*, as compared with the books and pamphlets of the day. Of the first number the original printing was 750 copies, which was close to the usual printing for a book or pamphlet at that time. But by 1814 the first volume had gone through ten editions, the seventh edition of volume ii came out the same year, and the eighth edition of volume iii the following year. By 1807 the original printings were around 5,000, and more were printed in subsequent editions. Few economic books or pamphlets of the period appeared in anywhere near as many copies as did the *Edinburgh Review*. Jeffrey's estimate in 1814 that the *Edinburgh Review* was read by 50,000 people within a month of publication was no idle boast, and when he wrote to Malthus in that year, regretting that Malthus had not put the material in his pamphlets on the Corn Laws into an article for the *Edinburgh Review*, he was probably understating the case when he said: 'You know they would be read there by twice as many people as ever see pamphlets.'

A principal reason for the establishment of the rival *Quarterly Review* under Tory auspices in 1809 was that the *Edinburgh* with its Whig political bias was going into so many Tory homes. Sir Walter Scott said of the *Edinburgh* in 1808, in connection with the plans to establish the *Quarterly Review*:*

> Of this work 9,000 copies are printed quarterly, and no genteel family *can* pretend to be without it, because, independent of its politics, it gives the only valuable literary criticism which can be met with. Consider, of the numbers who read this work, how many are there likely to separate the literature from the politics?—how many youths are there upon whose mind the flashy and bold character of the work is likely to make an indelible impression?—and think what the consequence is likely to be.

What Scott said of the political articles in the early *Edinburgh Review* was undoubtedly equally true of the economic articles. It is a reasonable assumption that Ricardo, albeit the most famous of those whose interest in economics was fired by the economic articles in the *Edinburgh Review*, was simply one of a great number whose interests were directed to economic problems by the writings in the *Edinburgh Review*

* *The Letters of Sir Walter Scott.* Edited by H. J. C. Grierson. London, 1932. vol. ii, p. 121.

that came from Horner's pen or that were inspired there by Horner's belief in the importance of economic analysis.

Horner's Articles in 'Edinburgh Review',
not here reprinted,
and other Anonymous Publications

Edinburgh Review

Christison's General Diffusion of Knowledge. — No. I, October 1802, xi.

The Trial of John Peltier, Esq., for a Libel Against Napoleon Bonaparte. — No. IV, July 1803, xviii.

Miss Williams's Political and Confidential Correspondence of Louis XVI. — No. V, October 1803, xvii.

Adams's Letters on Silesia. — No. IX, October 1804, xiv.

A Short Statement of Facts, relative to the Late Election of a Mathematical Professor in the University of Edinburgh. — No. XIII, October 1805, vii.

Translation of Mr. Fox's History. — No. XXIX, October 1809, xiii.

Leonhard Euler. *Elements of Algebra . . . translated from the French.* 2 vol. (London, 1797). Horner was the translator, and author of biographical sketch of Euler.

A Short Account of a Late Short Administration. (London, 1807.)

Special Report of The Directors of The African Institution, made at the Annual General Meeting on the 19th of April, 1815, respecting the Allegations made in a Pamphlet Entitled 'A Letter to William Wilberforce, Esq., by R. Thorpe, Esq., &c.' (London, 1815.)

Authority for Assignment of Authorship of 'Edinburgh Review'
Articles and other Publications to Francis Horner

All articles in the *Edinburgh Review* up to 1912 were anonymous. The economic articles here reprinted, and the other articles listed as by Horner, are attributed to him on the basis of information in the *Memoirs of Francis Horner*, or in the Horner papers at the London School of Economics. The list is identical with that in the *Dictionary of National Biography*, except that the *Dictionary* omits 'Playfair's Edition of Wealth of Nations,' and attributes to Horner 'Sir John Sinclair's Essays' in April 1803, which is also assigned to Horner by Leonard Horner, in the *Memoirs of Francis Horner*. The disagreement as to the authorship of this last article, which has also been attributed to Francis Jeffrey, is explained by a passage in an unpublished letter of May 11, 1803 from Horner to Jeffrey: 'I was a little surprised to find two pages of my writing upon that great subject, Sir John Sinclair; I thought I had burned it, but must have left it by accident in the book: there is an absurd incongruity in the transition to your style from mine, from my formality to your ease and vivacity—like a change from the dead march to the jig-step; like—but you will furnish such

20

similes as may be proper for the occasion.' Horner frequently sent on to Jeffrey from London books for review, and it is possible that there are other cases where Horner's notes were similarly incorporated in a review written by someone else. In another case, when Horner transmitted to Jeffrey a review by Henry Hallam—'Mrs. Trimmer on Lancaster's Plan of Education'—that apparently never was published, he wrote that he had 'added a page or two,' and it may be that articles whose authorship is unknown, or attributed to others, contain paragraphs or pages from the pen of Horner.

A more important point in doubt is whether Horner may not have written other economic articles whose authorship is still unknown. Letters to and from Jeffrey have references to a number of other books that Horner was thinking of reviewing, but there were many gaps between Horner's intentions and the completion of reviews. Two reviews on monetary problems that Horner talked of doing, and which subsequently appeared without any evidence as to authorship, were 'Foster on the Commercial Exchanges,' article viii in October 1806, and 'Wheatley on Money and Commerce,' article iii in July 1807. Horner may have written these, but it could be more easily conjectured (and no more than conjecture is possible) that the author was Brougham. Mr. Nowell C. Smith, in *The Letters of Sydney Smith*, attributes to Horner, but without supporting evidence, 'The Carnatic Question,' article xvii in January 1808. It is plausible, both on content and on style, that Horner should have written this, but lacking primary evidence I have not included it in the list of his articles. In 'The Authorship of Economic Articles in the *Edinburgh Review*, 1802–1847,' I discuss several other cases of articles that have been attributed to Horner, either in error or on questionable evidence.

The authority for attributing to Horner the 1797 translation of Euler's *Elements of Algebra*, and the writing of the biographical sketch of Euler, is the Advertisement, by John Hewlett, in the third English edition of 1822. Here Hewlett explains that Horner, under his supervision, did the translation while a student of Hewlett's, and wrote the sketch of Euler from material supplied by Hewlett. The third, and the two subsequent editions, carry a subtitle: *To Which is Prefixed a Memoir of the Life and Character of Euler by the late Francis Horner, Esq., M.P.*

The pamphlet *A Short Account of a Late Short Administration* appeared anonymously, but was generally known at the time to have been written by Horner, and was republished in his *Memoirs*.

The authority for assigning the 1815 pamphlet is a letter in the Horner papers from Henry Brougham to Leonard Horner in 1820: 'Are you aware of a . . . report of a Com^{tt}. of the African Institution in 1815—drawn up by him?' Circumstantial support is given to this statement by Brougham by the fact that Horner was active in Parliament in defending the African Institution against the same charges to which the pamphlet was an answer, and by his statement in Parliament that he was a member of the African Institution, and that 'He was

21

happy to add, however, that the African institution were about to submit to the public a statement, in which they were to refute, point by point, the allegations contained in this calumnious libel. (Hansard, vol. xxix, 1006, February 23, 1815.)

NOTE ON PRINCIPAL SOURCES*

The larger part of the material in this Introduction is based on *Memoirs and Correspondence of Francis Horner, M.P.*, edited by his brother Leonard Horner, 2 vol., 2d. edition (Boston and London, 1853), and on the Horner papers, owned by Lady Eleanor Langman, the grand-niece of Francis Horner, that are on deposit at the London School of Economics. *The Letters of Sydney Smith*, edited by Nowell C. Smith, 2 vol. (Oxford, 1953), Lord Cockburn's *Life of Lord Jeffrey with a Selection from His Correspondence*, 2 vol. (Edinburgh, 1852), and Cosmo Nelson Innes' *Memoir of Thomas Thomson, Advocate* (Edinburgh, 1854) have a number of letters relating to Horner's connection with the *Edinburgh Review*. Some of the discussion in the Introduction follows closely material in my article, 'The Authorship of Economic Articles in the *Edinburgh Review*, 1802–1847,' in *The Journal of Political Economy*, vol. lxi, June 1953, pp. 232–259. For the significance of Henry Thornton's *An Enquiry into the Nature and Effects of the Paper Credit of Great Britain*, I have drawn upon Professor Hayek's introduction to the 1939 Reprint (London and New York). *The Works and Correspondence of David Ricardo*, edited by Piero Sraffa with the collaboration of M. H. Dobb, 10 vol. (Cambridge, 1951–1955), furnished helpful background material, in addition to the letters quoted.

* The material used in the Introduction to this Reprint was collected in connection with a study of the British monetary and banking controversy from 1797 to the 1870's, for which I received aid from the Committee on Research Funds from the Graduate School of Northwestern University, and from the American Philosophical Society.

Vol. I ([No. I] Oct. 1802), Art. VII (pp. 61–63).
An Inquiry into the Causes and Effects of Emigration from the Highlands and Western Islands of Scotland; with Observations on the Means to be employed for preventing it. By Alexander Irvine, Minister of Ranoch. 1802.

THE opportunities which this clergyman must possess of local information, induced us to expect instruction on a very interesting topic in the political economy of Scotland. But the reverend author has preferred fine writing to inquiry; and his reader, who looks for facts, will in vain peruse a tedious volume of eloquence, that may not be altogether agreeable to his taste. For ourselves, we must confess, that we could not help feeling some degree of impatience, while we dutifully laboured through his toilsome declamation. But now that the task is over, we dismiss all irritation from our mind; and we not only can willingly forgive the honest, but mistaken, desire of giving delight and of gaining fame, but we feel ourselves likewise bound to pay our tribute of applause to that ardent patriotism which breathes throughout this piece of composition. We might not perhaps, without a little hesitation, adopt the expressions, or participate the wonder of Mr Irvine, when he speaks of emigration from the Highlands, as 'a singular phenomenon in the history of Britain, that so many citizens should leave *the most favoured* province.' But we acknowledge the eloquence at least of his remark, that, 'in a free-born mind, of the Celtic cast, there is *some quality* that glories to struggle and overcome adversity.' Being natives of a Lowland district, we must be excused by the local proprieties of our own patriotism, if we venture to doubt, whether he would prove successful in the issue of the following challenge: 'If you except Switzerland and the Valais, before the French revolution, I defy the most renowned kingdoms of Europe to adduce one province, that competes with the Highlands in point of national felicity.' We cannot, however, dissemble our admiration of the pious simplicity and gratitude of the following passage:

'It is well known that the Highlanders, scattered through our fleets and armies, arrest the admiration, and excite the astonishment of the world. Patient of hunger and fatigue, ready to obey, and as able to execute, they are selected for the most arduous and desperate enterprizes, and uniformly cover themselves with glory, though not always crowned with victory. Who can read the history of the dissensions, regarding the succession of the Queen of Hungary to the Imperial dignity—the war for the admission of the French and Russians into

23

Germany—the contests for the independence of America—the defence of the British settlements in India—and the late struggles with the French Republic—without thanking Providence that he was born a Highlander? Who can then learn, without regret, that those first in assault, and last in retreat, abandon their native country, and abandon its defence?' &c.

From the manner in which the subject is treated in this pamphlet, we have no proper opportunity of entering into any general remarks on the emigrations from Scotland. If it should be presented to us in a more manageable form, we shall seize the occasion with pleasure. The history of the Highland emigrations is intimately connected with that of the agricultural improvements of the island: and our interest is at present heightened, by the temporary effects that result from the recent cessation of hostilities. These consequences, indeed, are not confined to the Highlands. The general subject, considered as an article of political philosophy, might be illustrated by present examples from every district of the country, and from every department of industry. And the description of that conduct, which an enlightened government will pursue, with regard to emigration, would involve some of the most important principles of national policy, and some of the most sacred privileges of mankind.

Vol. I ([No. I] Oct. 1802), Art. XIV (pp. 106–108).
The Utility of Country Banks considered. London, 1802. pp. 86.

THESE eighty-six pages, of which not more than twenty are employed on the subject of country Banks, afford an amusing specimen of plagiarism. The anonymous author appears to have met with Hume's Political Discourses, and Smith's Inquiry, a short time, probably, before the date of his pamphlet, which is made up of unacknowledged extracts from those works, mutilated both in composition and argument, and thrown together into a shapeless mass. By a diligent study of those excellent models, for a certain number of years, he may perhaps qualify himself to understand such disquisitions; and, by the improvement at least of his taste, be prevented from violating, as he has done, the property of others.

In the following extract, our readers will easily recognize the fragments of a passage in Smith's chapter on the wages of labour; but they will also acknowledge, how much the tame sketches of one artist may be improved, when a new tone of colouring is imparted by the hand of a greater master.*

'All animals multiply, naturally, in proportion to their means of subsistence; and no species can ever multiply beyond it. In civilized society, the scantiness of subsistence among the lower ranks of the people, sets a limit to the multiplication of the human species, by destroying a great part of the children produced by their fruitful marriages. When labour is to be had, and is liberally rewarded, the lower orders are enabled to provide better for their children. A greater number is consequently reared, and added to the national stock of population. It necessarily does this, too, as nearly as possible in the proportion which the demand for labour requires. In this point of view, we may consider the institutions which tend to set it in motion: The *manufactures* of a country are, *inventions for* the multiplication of the human species, and *the propagation of intellectual beings; they are the creative powers of thought, happiness, and moral existence.* Without such fostering establishments, life would decay, and society wither at its root. With such aid, the demand for man increases, and the reward of labour necessarily encourages the marriages and multiplication of labourers; so that a continual increasing demand is supplied by a continually increasing population. An increase of wealth produces the liberal reward of labour, which is the cause of increasing population.

---

* [In the 2nd and 3rd editions the wording in the second clause of this sentence is: "how much the tame sketches of a great master may be improved, when a new tone of colouring is imparted by the hand of a bolder artist."]

25

To complain of it, is to lament over the necessary cause and effect of the greatest public prosperity.'

The manner in which the principles of the Wealth of Nations are mistated, is almost as ludicrous as this debasement of its composition. After copying the instances which Smith gives, of the various commodities that, in a rude state of commerce, perform the functions of money, our author adds the following example.

'We may add another, hitherto unnoticed, though not so clearly a species of exchange, which is manure, that children and poor persons gather on the post-roads in Yorkshire, and in the north, where, for the excellence of its quality, it is valuable to the farmer; and I am told that it is a very common practice for poor persons to exchange it for coals, or other necessaries; thus making horse dung a species of money.'

In another part of the pamphlet, we are promised the 'explanation of some phenomena which have surprised the reasoners on finance.' One of these phenomena is 'the increasing prosperity of the nation, during a long and expensive war.'—For the solution of which, he deems it quite enough to transcribe several pages, still without acknowledgment, of those reasonings by which Mr Smith shows that the expenses of foreign war may be defrayed by the exportation of the finer manufactures. What was, in fact, a particular mode of national expenditure, our pamphleteer conceives to have been an accession to the national wealth; and he explains 'the increasing prosperity of the nation, during a long and expensive war,' by a series of observations, which lead Smith himself to the very different conclusion, 'that manufactures may flourish amidst the ruin of their country, and begin to decay upon the return of its prosperity.'

Lest our readers should be misled, by us, to suppose that the whole of this tract is transcription, without any attempts at original composition, we have selected one or two passages, which we do not remember to have seen, either in the Wealth of Nations, or in the Political Discourses of Mr Hume.

'As grand political machines, moving the great levers of the empire, and raising the ponderous powers of war, National Banks may be contemplated as national bulwarks, towers of strength, and edifices of defence.'

'Building, though considerably checked during the war, has in many parts of the country proceeded with vigour; and houses, streets, and towns have been raised, as substantially, on paper currency, as brick or stone, cemented by gold or silver, could have built them.'

'If it be objected, that gold, the sight of which so gratifies the human eye, is now seldom to be seen, let it be remembered, that it is invisibly performing its magic effects on the commerce of the nation. We may

26

be assured, that every guinea, though unseen, is actively employed for the good of the community; its paper representative is not intended to supply its place, that it may sleep in idleness; on the contrary, it goes forth to seek new adventures: The chrysal of the day is not bred up in idleness; he seldom sleeps long in the iron chests of bankers.'

'When we consider the effects of an extended commerce, we may trace the twenty shilling note of a Glasgow bank, from its embarkation in the Clyde, in its form of manufacture, through the West or East Indies, till it returns, in the suite of a Nabob, who fixes it in a palace which he builds in the neighbourhood of his native city, on his return from Asia, whither he himself was probably first sent by the operation of paper currency.'

Vol. I ([No. I] Oct. 1802), Art. XXV (pp. 172–201).
*An Inquiry into the Nature and Effects of the Paper Credit of
Great Britain.* By Henry Thornton Esq. M.P. London, 1802.
pp. 320.

THE progress of commercial philosophy has been much accelerated by the writings of practical men of business. In that, as
well as in the other departments of civil knowledge, it is only from
the actual course of affairs that the statesman can derive his
maxims of policy, or the speculative inquirer deduce the conclusions of his science: but the habits of both are incompatible with
a personal knowledge of detail. It is necessary that the labour of
accumulating particular facts, should be separated from the more
liberal task of generalizing these into principles; and that they,
who are qualified to combine larger views, should be furnished, by
the minute accuracy of others, with descriptions in which they may
confide. In England, which is the native-country of political
œconomy, the works, contributed by professional men, form a
large deposite of authenticated facts. For these we are primarily
indebted to that diffused literature, which multiplies the demand
for varied information, and has already liberalized the practition-
ers in almost every walk of industry. But the greater number of
these publications have been suggested by such occasional events,
in the fluctuation of our commercial prosperity, as rouse a general
interest, and direct the curiosity of the public to that quarter of the
great machine, in which the derangement is supposed to have
taken place. It is in this manner, that every period of dearth has
contributed in some degree to alleviate subsequent years of scarcity,
by the instruction which it yielded against popular prejudice.
Those numerous tracts, in which alone the detailed history of our
foreign commerce can be traced, at least during its earlier progress,
appear to have been prompted by the frequent disturbance, which
the balance of exchanges suffered, from the alternations of war
and peace. The immediate consequences of the South Sea scheme,
and of the many wild projects which about the same time excited
such a pernicious rage, were somewhat compensated by the more
distinct knowledge, which they ultimately furnished, with respect
to the bounds of commercial adventure. It was in a similar manner, from the embarrassments, that were occasioned in the reign
of King William by the reformation of the coin, that our politicians
first derived a clear and steady light on the subject of metallic
circulation. And that curious system, by the operation of which
the use of precious coin is now almost superseded, had remained

in a great measure unknown to all but the bankers and traders of London, until the suspension of cash payments at the Bank of England produced that copious information, which, in various forms, has been communicated to the public,

Of all the publications, which that momentous event has occasioned, the most valuable unquestionably is this of Mr Thornton. With no ostentatious professions, and with no admixture of superfluous matter, it contains the largest portion of new information that has for a long time been offered to those, who, either for the pleasures of speculation, or with a view to public life, are engaged in the researches of political economy. The instruction, however, which may be derived from the work, is not to be obtained by a cursory or passive perusal. The author has so little management in the disposition of his materials, and is frequently so much embarrassed in the explanation of arguments, that his reader must undertake the trouble of reducing these to a more precise statement, as well as of digesting the general subject in a more distinct form. Even in point of accuracy, his reasonings are not to be trusted with the same confidence to which his information is entitled; for, if examined with care, they will sometimes be found defective: nor can it excite any surprise, that the same opportunities, by which a person has been eminently instructed in the facts of such a subject, should have proved unfavourable to those speculative habits, which exercise the powers of accurate and comprehensive inference. At the same time, from our own experience, we may caution the reader of Mr Thornton, that he should not too hastily consider as an erroneous deduction, what he may find to be only the confused statement of a just argument. For the work indicates, throughout, an author unpractised in composition. In most of the details separately taken, there is that degree of perspicuity and ease, which shows him to have been fully possessed of the subject; though he rarely attains precision and distinctness of expression. But the various discussions are so unskilfully arranged, that they throw no light on each other, and we can never seize a full view of the plan: so imperfectly is the order of investigation defined, that sometimes an inquiry is prematurely anticipated, sometimes inconveniently postponed; and the author has been frequently constrained, by his consciousness of this imperfection, to repeat the same disquisition in different places. These defects appear to have arisen, in some measure, from his having varied his design, after he was engaged in the execution of the work; for he tells us that his first intention —'was merely to expose some popular errors which related chiefly to the suspension of the cash payments of the Bank of England, and to the influence of our paper currency on the price of provisions. But in pursuing his purpose, many questions occurred which it seemed important to discuss, partly on account of their having some bearing on the topics under consideration, and partly because they appeared to be of general importance, and had either been left unexplained, or had been inaccurately stated by those English writers who have treated of paper credit. This work has therefore assumed, in some degree, the character of a general treatise.'—*Introd.*

It is to be regretted that it did not receive in every respect the form, as it contains the valuable substance, of a general treatise. Most of the prolixity, and some of the obscurity, which oppress the reader in its present shape, would have been avoided, if the temporary topics, which formed his original object, had been sunk into a subordinate digression, instead of being suffered to interweave themselves with more general inquiries through the whole train of the discourse. Adhering to this distinction, we shall attempt an abstract of its principal contents: and that we may observe an order which will both afford a clear view of his doctrine, and admit of such remarks being introduced as we think necessary, we shall consider, *first*, The principles which he has adopted on the general theory of paper credit; *secondly*, His account of that system of credit and of paper-money which is established in this country; *thirdly*, His explanation of the difficulties to which the Bank of England was subjected in 1797; and *fourthly*, His opinion with regard to the influence of our present paper currency upon the present state of prices.

I. Although some general truths, respecting the operations of paper money, have been ascertained, the analysis of that very intricate subject is far from being complete. Even the fundamental principles are still involved in some degree of obscurity, and writers of equal authority have thus been led to vary in many of their deductions. It may be useful, therefore, to present a full view of the opinions which are professed by Mr Thornton. In this, we shall not entirely confine ourselves to the three preliminary chapters, in which he has attempted to arrange his general doctrine; because several of the most important principles are not developed in that sketch, but receive an incidental explanation in the course of his subsequent reasonings.

1. The origin, and the solid foundation of every system of paper-money, Mr Thornton has correctly placed in that credit, which subsists among commercial men with regard to their mercantile transactions. By this mutual trust, they are brought under pecuniary engagements to each other; and it is the expression of these engagements in writing, that creates the first and largest

portion of circulating paper. By reducing them to a written form, the insecurity, that attends verbal obligations, is avoided by the creditor; and an advantage is obtained, on the other hand, by the debtor, in having that confidence, which is entertained both of his funds and of his prudence, expressed in a regular and transmissible document. Promissory notes and bills of exchange, as such documents have been called, were soon discovered to be susceptible of a more extended use, than that of recovering debts to the original creditor. They admitted, like other instruments of debt, and more easily than most others, of being transferred; and, in consequence of this facility, they came gradually to circulate as a representative of value, that is, as an effective medium of exchange, in almost all payments of a large amount. After their utility in this function had been ascertained, it was an obvious improvement to adapt them, by a small change of their form, to those ordinary payments in which the precious metals had always been employed; and to substitute, by this simple contrivance, a very cheap instrument of commerce in the place of a very expensive one. The promissory notes of bankers, which are payable on demand, have accordingly for a long time past performed, in this country, the ordinary purposes of exchange in almost all transactions of a small amount, as well as in settling the small balances of larger transactions.

This description of circulating paper differs, in one material circumstance, from the opinion of Mr Boyd, who, in his recent publication, has expressly denied that bills of exchange, or any other negotiable paper, form a part of the circulating medium. 'The latter (Mr Boyd has said) is the circulator; the former are merely objects of circulation.' This verbal antithesis, it may be remarked, is calculated to suggest a very erroneous principle; for, even in theory, no definite boundary can be marked between the circulating medium and the commodities of which it facilitates the exchange. The language of Mr Thornton is more consistent with a just view of the subject. All negotiable paper is, by its form, the representative of value; and is therefore qualified, more or less perfectly, according to its varieties of form, to serve the purposes of money. It is convertible into cash; and on the faith of this convertibility it passes immediately as cash. The precious metals themselves do not pass as money, except on the faith of their convertibility into commodities. Paper-money, in one form, may circulate less quickly than in another, and may not be so readily convertible into specie; but its essential character is the same. Not to mention those bills drawn upon London, by which all the great payments of our foreign and domestic commerce are

31

effected; a vast number of smaller bills circulate among the traders of the country, who successively indorse them to each other. While some of these are from day to day withdrawn, they are continually replaced by others; and the average number of such bills, floating in the general market at once, forms unquestionably a portion of the circulating medium. By omitting them, we should leave ourselves a very imperfect idea both of the extent, and of the consequential operations, of our paper system.

2. In common with all other writers, Mr Thornton appears to admit, that the convertibility of paper into specie is the basis upon which that system must be founded. He is not indeed quite explicit; and there is much reason to regret, that he has not been at more pains to elucidate this principle, and the limitations with which the statement of it may be qualified. That the immediate convertibility of paper into gold is an indispensable condition of its credit, as we are taught by the language of system, has been disproved by the recent history of the Bank of England; which has happily quieted the apprehensions, to which our best-informed politicians yielded, on account of the event of 1797. The maintenance of credit during a short interval of suspended payments, was a case, indeed, which might have been foreseen from theory, and was not wholly unknown to our previous experience. But that a restriction of this kind should have been continued for more than five years, without any depreciation of the paper from a failure of confidence, is a fact which has falsified all reasonable prediction, and forms an exception to the most confident maxims of all former economists. It is incumbent on us, therefore, to consider how far we are required to limit, by the result of this experiment, a principle which had been generalized prematurely. In this, we receive slight assistance from Mr Thornton.*

The convertibility of paper into specie, without delay and without loss, may be necessary in two respects: to maintain the credit of the paper, by precluding that depreciation which proceeds from a failure of confidence; and to preserve the value of the paper from that depreciation, which originates in an excess of circulating medium. The necessity of immediate access to gold, for the credit of the paper, may be superseded, it appears, by a full persuasion on the part of the public that the paper is secured by ample funds. But this can have no effect in restricting the quantity, which is, on the contrary, encouraged by this very confidence of the public. Mr Thornton, accordingly, expresses his opinion, that gold coin is the standard by which the value of all paper money must be regulated; and that, in order to maintain an uniformity between

* Pp. 70. 187. 258. 279.

32

them, there should always be a considerable fund of bullion in the country, and a certain degree of interchange of the paper for precious coin. This principle is so implicated with all the investigations of his treatise, and is of itself so important, that we are sorry he did not think of illustrating it more fully, and of reducing it, if possible, to more specific terms.

3. He has explained, however, with great clearness, another part of the theory of money; the different effects of a quick or a slow circulation. Such of our readers, as have attended to the history of opinions in political science, will recollect that a consideration, which now seems quite obvious, was long overlooked by the most acute and profound inquirers. Montesquieu and Hume fell into several mistakes, from not adverting to the degree in which the representative power of money is augmented, by a more rapid transmission; and although the principle may be alluded to, in a few passages of Smith's work, he appears to have been unaware of its extent. We doubt if even the writers, by whom it has been more recently urged, have traced all the effects of its operation.

The quantity of money, necessary for performing a certain number of exchanges in a certain time, may be considered as nearly in the inverse ratio of its velocity of circulation. Whatever, therefore, tends to accelerate the general rate, contributes, so long as the number of exchanges remains unaugmented, to economize the necessary quantity. And if, by the operation of any cause, its movement be retarded, the want of an additional quantity will be felt. From the same proposition it likewise follows, that, if one kind of money is susceptible of a more rapid circulation than another, a smaller quantity will be required of the former than of the latter, to carry on a given number of exchanges in a given time.

Mr Thornton has justly observed,* that, in a commercial country, whatever the circulating medium consists of, it is apt to vary in its rate of circulation. A high and prosperous state of mercantile confidence quickens it; and it is apt to be retarded, during the intervals of distrust and alarm. Every merchant, who lies under pecuniary engagements, must not only arrange the punctual fulfilment of these, but must reserve a farther provision against contingencies. During an interval of alarm, he of course makes this reserve rather greater than in ordinary times; and at a period of great confidence, he ventures to keep it rather less. We shall perceive, in the sequel, what application Mr Thornton has made of these deductions.

He has likewise observed,† with regard to paper money in particular, that some kinds of paper circulate more slowly than others.

* P. 47. † P. 41.

33

Bills of exchange, for example, bear interest, and become daily more valuable to the holder. Bank notes, on the contrary, like guineas, occasion a daily loss to the possessor, because no interest accrues. There is thus a reason for detaining the one, and for parting with the other as soon as possible. Commercial people will endeavour to keep their necessary provision for future payments, rather in bills, than in bank notes.

4. The most important, perhaps, of all questions respecting the operations of paper money, relates to its effect upon the price of commodities. Mr Thornton admits, in the most explicit manner, that, in this particular, there is no difference between a currency of paper and one consisting of the precious metals; and that in both cases, if the quantity of circulating medium is permanently augmented, without a corresponding augmentation of internal trade, a rise will unavoidably take place in the price of exchangeable articles. Indeed this is a principle, upon which all the writers on commerce, both practical and speculative, are agreed: they have thought it so undeniable, as to require no particular illustration; and have rather assumed it as an obvious truth, than as a proposition which depended on inference. On this idea is founded Mr Hume's well-known argument against banks; and it is equally implied in Smith's satisfactory confutation of that objection: it forms the foundation of those presumptions, from which Mr Boyd has lately inferred an improper increase of Bank of England paper; and it is implicitly admitted likewise by Mr Thornton, one great object of whose book is to persuade the public that there has been no such increase.

Dr Smith, our readers will recollect, has refuted Mr Hume's notion, that paper-money raises prices, by referring to what he considers as a general fact in the theory of circulation; that every addition of paper to the currency displaces an equivalent quantity of gold. From different parts of Mr Thornton's work a few remarks may be collected, which place this principle in a more correct point of view. The language, in which Smith has described the displacement of gold, is not calculated to convey a very distinct conception of the manner in which it really takes place. The quantity of goods in the market (he says) being precisely the same after the paper is issued as before, the same quantity of money will be sufficient to circulate them: the channel of circulation remaining precisely the same, whatever is poured into it beyond the sum that is sufficient to fill it, cannot run in it, but must overflow: the sum that overflows is too valuable to lie unemployed at home; it will therefore be sent abroad; and, as the paper cannot

34

go abroad, the gold will be exported.* If this statement be literally understood, it involves a statement which is contrary to historical fact; for, by what process did the discovery of the American mines operate upon prices, except by causing a much greater quantity of money to run in the channel of circulation, than had previously been sufficient to circulate the same quantity of goods? Mr Thornton has justly remarked, that the channel of circulation can never be said to be full, because employment is still afforded to a larger quantity of circulating medium by means of an advanced price of goods. 'This advanced price of goods is the same thing as a reduced price of coin: the coin, therefore, in consequence of its reduced price, is carried out of the country for the sake of obtaining for it a better market.'† Thus, the immediate effect of an addition to the paper currency, is a rise of prices, which leads to an exportation of gold. The gold is not immediately displaced, because the circulating medium admits of no augmentation; nor thrown out of the channel of circulation, because that can hold no more; nor sent abroad, because it would otherwise have been altogether unemployed at home. Dr Smith, it is evident, overlooked the intermediate event; and, because the real explanation did not suggest itself, had recourse to the exceptionable style of metaphorical description.—Mr Thornton has another remark,‡ which suggests a just correction of that general position, by which we exclude altogether any permanent operation of paper money in raising prices, while there is gold in circulation that may be displaced. The same exportation of gold, which remedies the temporary rise that takes place in the particular country where paper has been issued, has a tendency to increase the supply of precious metal in the general market of the world, and thus to occasion a general rise of prices in which that particular country must participate. The whole quantity of bullion, of which Great Britain has spared the use by adopting a different medium of domestic exchange, is added to the general stock of the mercantile commonwealth, as much as if an equal quantity had been brought additionally from America; and the saving of that annual loss, which would have been occasioned by the waste of British coin, is equivalent to an increase in the annual produce of the mines.— But, on the other hand, it must be remembered, that the use of paper money tends, in some degree, to *lower* the price of commodities. In proportion as the instruments of commerce, or the machinery of manufactures, are of a less expensive construction, the articles, which they contribute to produce, may be afforded at

* Wealth of Nations, I. p. 436.   † P. 211.   ‡ P. 304.

a lower rate. To employ paper money instead of gold, is to substitute a very cheap instrument of commerce in the room of a very expensive one. That system of credit, also, of which the limits are greatly extended by the use of paper, tends, as Mr Thornton has observed,* to reduce prices, both by enlarging competition, and by saving the trouble and expense of weighing, counting, and transporting money. The larger transactions of commerce are, by these means, greatly facilitated; and in this instance, as in every other, it is the true interest of the consumer that merchants should be permitted to adopt their own plans of economy.

Although, with these modifications, he admits the position of Dr Smith, that successive additions of paper to the currency will successively displace equivalent portions of gold, this must evidently cease to be true when the circulating medium already consists almost entirely of paper. In such circumstances the successive augmentations that may take place, are not compensated by any corresponding diminution in another part of the circulation; and the rise of prices, that immediately ensues, is not reduced by a subsequent exportation of gold. While the currency remains in this augmented state, without an increase of trade to absorb the excess, prices will remain high; and if the quantity of paper should still be continually increased, the prices of commodities will continue to rise. The price of bullion must be affected in the same manner, as that of every other article. And in a country, where a system of paper currency has gradually supplanted an ancient system of gold coin, the market price of gold bullion may thus come to exceed that price which was adopted, under the ancient system, by the regulations of the mint.

We perfectly agree with Mr Thornton, that, in a country where gold constitutes an indefinitely small portion of the circulating medium, an excessive issue of paper will raise the market price of gold above its mint price. But the manner, in which he has described the process by which this is effected, appears to us so erroneous, that we shall lay before our readers the passage in which he has explained his opinion. It is rather long for an extract: But it forms a detached dissertation complete in itself; and we could not easily have selected a shorter passage, that would have afforded so just a specimen of the author's general manner. It is unnecessary to point out to our readers, by particular references, the familiar perspicuity with which the facts are separately stated, and the perplexity with which they are combined into a train of reasoning.

'I proceed, in the next place, to show in what manner a general rise

* P. 315. and p. 17.

in the cost of commodities, whether proceeding from an extravagant issue of paper, or from any other circumstance, contributes to produce an excess of the market price above the mint price of gold.

'It is obvious, that, in proportion as goods are rendered dear in Great Britain, the foreigner becomes unwilling to buy them, the commodities of other countries, which come into competition with ours, obtaining a preference in the foreign market; and, therefore, that, in consequence of a diminution of orders from abroad, our exports will be diminished; unless we assume, as we shall find it necessary to do, that some compensation in the exchange is given to the foreigner for the disadvantage attending the purchase of our articles. But, not only will our exports lessen, in the case supposed; our imports also will increase: for the high British price of goods, will tempt foreign commodities to come in, nearly in the same degree in which it will discourage British articles from going out. I mean only, that these two effects (that of a diminished export, and that of an increased import) will follow, provided that we suppose, what is not supposable, namely, that, at the time when the price of goods is greatly raised in Great Britain, the course of exchange suffers no alteration. For the following reason, I have said, that this is not supposable. Under the circumstances which have been described, of a diminished export, and an increased import, the balance of trade must unavoidably turn against us; the consequence of which must be, that the drawers of bills on Great Britain, in foreign countries, will become more in number than the persons having occasion to remit bills. This disparity between the number of individuals wanting to draw, and of those wanting to remit, as was remarked in a former chapter, must produce a fall in the price at which the overabundant bills on England fell in the foreign market. The fall in the selling price, abroad, of bills payable here, will operate as an advantage to the foreign buyer of our commodities in the computation of the exchangeable value of that circulating medium of his own country, with which he discharges the debt in Britain contracted by his purchase. It will thus obviate the dearness of our articles: it will serve as a compensation to the foreigner, for the loss which he would otherwise sustain by buying in our market. The fall of our exchange, will therefore promote exportation, and encourage importation. It will, in a great degree, prevent the high price of goods in Great Britain from producing that unfavourable balance of trade, which, for the sake of illustrating the subject, was supposed to exist.

'The compensation thus made to the foreigner, for the high British price of all articles, is necessary, as an inducement to him to take them; somewhat in the same manner as a drawback, or bounty on exportation, is the necessary inducement to take those particular goods, which have been rendered too dear for the foreign market, by taxes laid on them in this country. In each case, the British consumer pays the high price, and the foreigner is spared, because otherwise he will not accept our commodities.

'The fall in our exchange was just now defined to be an advantage

37

gained in the computation of the exchangeable value of that foreign circulating medium with which the foreigner discharges his debt in Great Britain, a debt paid in the circulating medium of this country. It implies, therefore, a high valuation of his circulating medium, and a low valuation of ours; a low valuation, that is to say, both of our paper and of the coin which is interchanged with it.

'Now, when coin is thus rendered cheap, it by no means follows, that bullion is rendered cheap also. Coin is rendered cheap through its constituting a part of our circulating medium; but bullion does not constitute a part of it. Bullion is a commodity, and nothing but a commodity; and it rises and falls in value, on the same principle as all other commodities. It becomes, like them, dear, in proportion as the circulating medium for which it is exchanged is rendered cheap; and cheap, in proportion as the circulating medium is rendered dear.

'In the case, therefore, which has now been supposed, we are to consider coin as sinking below its proper and intrinsic worth, while bullion maintains its natural and accustomed price. Hence there arises that temptation, which was formerly noticed, either to convert back into bullion, and then to export; or, which is the same thing, to export, and then convert back into bullion; or, which is also the same thing, to convert back into bullion, and then sell to the Bank, at the price which would be gained by exportation, that gold which the Bank has purchased, and has converted from bullion into coin.

'In this manner, an increase of paper, supposing it to be such as to raise the price of commodities in Britain above the price at which, unless there is some allowance afforded in the course of exchange, they will be received in foreign countries, contributes to produce an excess of the market price above the mint price of gold, and to prevent, therefore, the introduction of a proper supply of it into the Bank of England, as well as to draw out of its coffers, that coin which the directors of the Bank would wish to keep in them.' p. 200.*

Although the whole of this long passage is professedly employed, to explain in what manner an increase of paper produces an excess of the market price of gold above its mint price, a sufficient explanation of that fact is distinctly given in a single sentence of the fifth paragraph: Bullion, like all other commodities, becomes dear in proportion as the circulating medium, for which it is exchanged, is rendered cheap. No other account of the fact can be given; and no farther explanation will be required. Our author, however,

* In a subsequent passage, the doctrine is thus summed up—'Let the manner in which an extravagant issue of notes operates, in producing the excess, be recollected. It raises, and probably by slow degrees, the cost of British goods. It thus obstructs the export of them, unless a compensation for the high price is afforded to the foreign buyer, in the rate of exchange; and the variation in our exchange produces a low valuation of our coin, compared with that of bullion. The state of the exchange, then, is the immediate cause of the evil in question.' p. 242. The reader, who may wish to verify our criticisms by examining the original work, will find the same doctrine urged, pp. 271 & 281.

has intermingled with this the statement of another very different fact; that fall of the foreign exchange, which might be expected to follow an excessive increase of our paper-money, and of which he seems to have formed an erroneous conception. The mistakes, which are involved in the preceding disquisition, appear to have arisen from his overlooking the distinction, of which in other parts of the work he is aware, between the bullion or general price of goods, and their local price in paper-currency. When the bullion price of our goods rises, that oscillation of the commercial balance, which Mr Thornton has imperfectly described, will certainly be produced, by the tendency of an unfavourable exchange to encourage exports, and by the reciprocal tendency of an increased exportation to restore the equilibrium of exchanges. But it is not the bullion price of goods that is raised by an increase of paper-money; which only occasions a rise in the *paper* or *currency* price, and occasions that sort of rise in the price of bullion as well as in that of all other commodities. The bullion price of these will remain, therefore, precisely the same; and although our goods acquire at home a nominal increase of value, they are not rendered dearer to the foreign merchant, who pays for them ultimately in that bullion which is the common measure of his currency and ours. In this point of view, the increase of paper-money appears to have no effect on the balance of exports and imports. There can be no doubt, however, that it will, notwithstanding, have a considerable effect on the apparent course of exchange. By that increase, our currency sinks in its bullion value, and a given sum of it will no longer purchase the same quantity of bullion: but the foreign currency, which is not supposed to have undergone a change, preserves its own bullion value; and a given sum of that will still purchase the same quantity of bullion as before. The proportion, therefore, of the bullion value of our currency to the bullion value of foreign currency, is altered; and, in order to preserve the same apparent rate of exchange, there ought to be a corresponding alteration of the numerical tables in which that rate is expressed. As long as the ancient mode of computation remains still in use, the apparent or computed rate of exchange will be different from the real one; and, whatever may be the actual state of credit or debt, the exchange will always be calculated so much less in our favour, or so much more against us, in proportion to the depreciation which has taken place in the bullion value of our currency. Our general exchanges might thus appear unprosperous, at the very time that the balance of trade was greatly in our favour; and if the issue of paper continued to increase, the exchange would appear to become more and more unfavourable, although the balance of exports and imports had remained unaltered. The difference, therefore, between the two cases, which Mr Thornton appears to have confounded, is very distinct. When the local rise of the price of goods consists in an actual increase of their bullion price, a real fall of the foreign exchange will generally take place, and will *occasion*, by the demand for bullion to be exported, a fluctuating excess of the market price above the mint price of gold. But when an excessive issue of paper money produces a nominal rise of prices, a nominal fall of the foreign exchange will always take place, and is a *consequence* of that steady excess of the market price of gold above its mint price, which originated immediately in the excessive issue of paper. The importance of the error, into which we imagine Mr Thornton to have fallen, will justify the length of these observations; to which we shall only add, that the operation of an excessive paper-currency, upon prices and upon the course of exchange, must be the same as that of a debasement of the coin, either by waste, or by the recent fraud of government.*

5. We shall conclude this first part of our abstract with some criticisms on another passage, in which Mr Thornton has not given a very satisfactory confutation of a popular prejudice, which however prevails so much, that the real fallacy of it ought to be explained.

'Some persons are of opinion, that, when the custom of buying on credit is pushed very far, and a great quantity of individual dealings is in consequence carried on by persons having comparatively little property, the national commerce is to be considered as unsupported by a proper capital; and that a nation, under such circumstances, whatever may be its ostensible riches, exhibits the delusive appearance of wealth.

'It must, however, be remembered, that the practice of buying on credit, in the internal commerce of the country, supposes the habit of selling on credit also to subsist; and to prevail, on the whole, in an exactly equal degree. In respect to the foreign trade of a country, the practice of dealing on credit indicates poverty or riches, in proportion as the credit generally taken is longer or shorter than the credit given. The custom which tradesmen have of selling to the consumers on credit, is also an indication of wealth in the commercial world: the traders must possess a surplus of wealth, either their own or borrowed, which bears an exact proportion to the amount of debts due to them by the consumers. Thus, that practice of trading on credit which prevails among us, so far as it subsists between trader and trader, is an indication

---

* See the Wealth of Nations, II. p. 215. (This important distinction, and the argument that is here founded upon it, we have since taken an opportunity of illustrating more at large, in the Review, in the Review of Lord King's Tract. See No. IV, Art. XI.) [This passage in brackets was added in the Fourth Edition.]

neither of wealth nor of poverty in the mercantile body; so far as it respects our transactions with foreign countries, it is an indication of extraordinary wealth belonging to the merchants of Great Britain; and so far as it respects the trade between the retailer and the consumer, implies a deficiency of wealth in the consumers, and a proportionate surplus of it among commercial men. The existing customs imply, that, on the whole, there is among our traders a great abundance of wealth.' p. 18.

This passage has all the formality of analytical reasoning, but furnishes no answer to the objection which the author professes to obviate; for no inference, against that objection, can be derived from the distinctions which he has marshalled in such methodical order. Overlooking, in his attempt to dispel a popular error, the real misconception from which it proceeds, he has unwarily assumed another principle no less fallacious. The credit, which this country gives to foreigners, is unquestionably the consequence of accumulated capital; but we have no proof of the assertion, that the credits of our home trade are equalized; and we are quite unable to understand his inference, that the credit, which traders allow to the consumers, implies in the latter a deficiency of wealth. But it is unnecessary to examine these positions more closely, because we have no doubt, that the balance of credits would be found, as a measure of national wealth, no less erroneous, and still more unmanageable, than that estimate of the precious metals which was long ago abandoned. At any rate, a more direct mode must be sought of correcting the very false opinion, that a nation, in which the system of commercial credit is established, 'exhibits only a delusive appearance of wealth.'

It is the operation of credit, not directly to augment the national capital, but to distribute it among those who undertake to employ it productively. The actual state of credit, therefore, does not indicate the amount of that capital, but the manner in which it is distributed. At different times, a part of the national capital may be entrusted in the hands of traders more or less qualified to employ it prudently, and in that respect it may occasionally be exposed to a less or greater degree of hazard. During a period of excessive confidence, therefore, instead of considering 'the national commerce as unsupported by a proper capital,' we are to consider a part of the national capital as injudiciously employed. The imprudent investiture of loans, however, is evidently a very different thing from the creation of fictitious capital. The latter cannot be effected by mercantile credit; and the former is an evil, which, though the system is occasionally liable to it, can never be of very long duration. That system is reared up, by the necessities of

4   41

commerce, for the most effective employment of capital; and those necessities adjust it, with tolerable exactness, between the limits of enterprise and caution. Wherever it has long been established to a great extent, there cannot be a more unequivocal proof, both of the solidity of the national capital, and of the prudence as well as skill with which it is employed.

II. Such, unquestionably, must be the conviction of every person, who puts himself in possession of the information that is contained in Mr Thornton's book, with respect to the present circumstances of our own country. It is upon this branch of the subject, that his communications are most satisfactory. The details might indeed have been rendered still more minute, without violating the consistency of his plan; but students of political philosophy will highly value the sketch, rude as it is, which he has drawn of our established system. While nothing can more immediately contribute, than the publicity of that system, in all its operations, to extend and strengthen the confidence on which it is solidly built: such dissected exhibitions of our commercial economy prepare, with necessary knowledge, those more active citizens who undertake the discussion of the national counsels. And the speculative politician, in receiving the legitimate materials of his science, may applaud the diligence that secures, while the original is yet entire, a delineation of that structure, which, after the revolutions of trade, will be seen only in the records of history. We shall attempt no more than a superficial outline of the description that might be formed out of Mr Thornton's materials.

The Bank of England may be considered as the main-spring of that complicated mechanism, by which the commercial payments of this country are transacted; and by which that comparatively small sum of money, with which they are performed, is kept in perpetual and regular circulation. The subordinate parts of this machine consist of about 70 private banking houses in London, and about 386 banks dispersed over the country. By the joint operation of these various money dealers, almost all large payments, founded on commercial bargains, are ultimately settled in London, with the money which issues from the bank of England. This money consists, in ordinary times, partly of precious coin, partly of bank notes. From its large capital and extended issue of paper, that Bank indirectly supplies the whole kingdom with as much gold as is required for circulation. Its notes are issued in loans, granted either for the accommodation of the public treasury, or for that of merchants by discount of their bills; and in consequence of a common agreement among the bankers, no notes of any private house are current in London. All the large payments of that metropolis are, in this manner, effected by the paper of the Bank of England; and they are chiefly transacted by the private bankers, who, according to a conjectural estimate, make daily payments to the amount of four or five millions, and have probably in their hands a very large proportion of the whole of the notes circulating in the metropolis.*

The commerce of London itself is immense, not only as a seat of populous and luxurious consumption, but as a station of manufactures, and an emporium of maritime trade. The number of payments, occasioned by such various transactions, is farther increased by the dividends which the national creditors receive on the great sum of our public debt. But in addition to all these payments, originating within the capital itself, bills are drawn upon London, and remittances are sent there to provide for them, from all quarters of the kingdom. Even foreign drafts, on account of merchants in the country, are, with scarcely any exceptions, made payable in London. And thus a great proportion of the pecuniary engagements, to which the whole commerce of the kingdom gives birth, are ultimately settled there.†

This transference of the country payments to London, has, in some degree, subsisted for a long time; the practice, once begun, was likely, from its great advantages, to be gradually extended; and of late years it seems to have been reduced to a regular and very commodious system. It was much facilitated by the multiplication of country banks, during that period of high prosperity and confidence which immediately preceded the late war. The formation of these, all over the country, was actively encouraged by the private bankers of London; and indeed the existence of a great national bank, which, like that of England, must provide a constant reservoir of gold, naturally suggests the creation of smaller establishments. Upon the formation of such banks in the country, many traders of all descriptions, who had formerly maintained a direct correspondence with merchants in London, fell into the practice of transacting their business with the metropolis, through the banker in their own neighbourhood, with whom they kept their cash. On their account, he drew largely upon a banker in London; who agreed to execute the extensive country business he had thus acquired, at a much lower commission, than what had formerly been paid by the several country traders to their separate correspondents. The rate of commission was reduced, in consequence of the diminished trouble as well as

* Pp. 60. 74. 154.
† P. 59.

43

risk: the labour of keeping accounts, writing letters, receiving and paying bills, was now transferred to one house, which had before then been divided among many; and a new security was afforded to the transactions between the metropolis and the country, by the interposed credit of wealthy and respectable country banks.*

The establishment of such a system of banks, and the transference of ultimate payments to one particular place, are in the natural course of that progressive subdivision of labour, which extends itself over an opulent and industrious country. The receipt and payment of money, instead of being conducted at home, are transferred, by every trader, to his banker; who devises means both of abridging his own labour, and of economizing the use of money, especially of that costly part of it which consists of specie. By his skill and success in attaining these objects, he manages an important part of trade, at an expense far inferior to what the merchants themselves must have incurred, had they continued to conduct it separately by their own clerks. In proportion, likewise, as the amount and number of payments and receipts is augmented in one particular place, the business of paying and receiving is more easily and cheaply transacted: the guineas or bank notes required, though more upon the whole, are fewer in proportion to the sums paid and received. So complete, accordingly, and so systematic is that economy in the use of notes, which long experience has introduced among the London bankers, that the present payments of that metropolis could scarcely be transacted, with due regularity, if the quantity of notes were to suffer any considerable diminution. In this, they are assisted by the fitness of bills of exchange and government securities to supply the place of bank notes: for the interest, that grows on such negotiable paper while it is detained, saves all the loss which the banker would undergo from the detention of coin or notes; and there is a certain sort and quantity of bills, on the conversion of which into money, he may rely almost as confidently as on the changing of a note into guineas, or of a guinea into silver. The ingenuity of these money-dealers, in sparing the circulating medium, is aptly illustrated by a custom which prevails among the city bankers. Each of them sends a clerk, at an appointed hour in the afternoon, to a room provided for their use. Each clerk there exchanges the drafts on other bankers received at his own house, for the drafts on his own house received at the houses of other bankers. The balances of the several bankers are transferred from one to another, in a manner which it is unnecessary to explain in detail, and the several balances are finally wound up by each clerk

* Pp. 60. 155. 160.

44

into one balance. The difference between the whole sum which each banker has to pay to all other city bankers, and the whole sum which he has to receive from all other city bankers, is, therefore, all that is discharged in bank notes or money; a difference, evidently, much less in its amount than that to which the several differences would be equal.*

But the economized use of circulating medium is by no means the only collateral advantage, that arises from this system of banks, connected in subordination to each other, with the great national Bank at their head. Although a very few of the country establishments have occasionally subjected themselves to the charge of encouraging rash speculation, the system, in its complex operation, has a real tendency to strengthen as well as to enlarge the basis of credit. Bankers possess, from their situation, very superior means of distinguishing the careful trader from the improvident. The bill transactions of the neighbourhood pass under their inspection; and by this information they are enabled to measure out confidence very nearly in a just proportion. In fact, it is considered as a regular branch of their professional experience, that they should appreciate the credit of the various traders within their district of circulation; and this sort of practical sagacity they are understood to cultivate with great assiduity. It is said to be the general practice of banks, to communicate such intelligence for their mutual advantage. Each of them endeavours to limit, not only the sum which any one trader shall obtain from themselves, but the total amount also, so far as they are able, of the sum which the same person shall borrow in different places. They endeavour, above all, to discourage bills of accommodation. While the transactions of country traders are thus surveyed by the banks of their respective districts, those of the country banks themselves are subject to the view of the London bankers, their correspondents; and these, again, are in some degree controuled by the Bank of England, which restricts, according to its own discretion, the credit with which they are accommodated. A series of checks is thus maintained, which, though far from establishing a complete security against all injurious speculation, presents a powerful obstacle to its progress.†

But the Bank of England retains another check, of a highly important nature, over the banks in the country. The issue of its own notes is restricted, in ordinary times, by the obligation to convert them into specie. The quantity of country paper, even during the present times, is limited by its accustomed convertibility

* Pp. 28. 39. 55. *note.* 60. 75. 164.
† P. 165.

45

into the notes of the Bank of England. This is the opinion of Mr Boyd* as well as of Mr Thornton; but the latter has more minutely explained the manner, in which he conceives the effect to be produced. If a particular country banker is imprudent enough to issue an extraordinary quantity of paper, while that of the Bank of England does not exceed the demands of London circulation, a local rise of prices will be produced within the district of that country paper, but prices in London will remain as before. In this situation, the holders of country paper, in order that they may purchase goods where they are cheaper, will return that paper to the banker, demanding in return Bank of England notes, or at least bills upon London. The excess of his notes will thus be continually returned upon the country banker, and he will at length find himself under the necessity of limiting his issue to that quantity, which the circulation of his own district can absorb. The quantity of Bank of England paper may thus be said to regulate the quantity of that which is issued by the country banks. It is not, that one uniform ratio is maintained between these two quantities; but that both are in the same proportion to the demand that is created for each, by the trade which it is destined to circulate. Whenever the Bank of England paper happens to exceed what is required for the purposes of London circulation, the country paper may become excessive in the same degree. And such an excess of Bank of England paper may be produced, either by a diminution in the number of payments, while that of notes remains undiminished; or by whatever has a tendency, while the number of payments remains unaugmented, to augment the number or the effective power of the notes in circulation.†

Having taken this general survey of our system of credit and circulation in its ordinary state, while its movements are regular, we shall now direct our attention to the disorders of which it is occasionally susceptible, either from external accident, or from inherent defects. In consequence of the mutual connexion that subsists among its parts, and the subordination of all to the Bank of England, those disorders sometimes pervade the whole system, and embarrass the operations even of the great establishment at the head. It is of national importance, that that body should be ready to adopt, under the pressure of such circumstances, an enlightened and salutary policy.

How solidly soever the foundations of mercantile credit may be laid, both in public confidence and in the real security of responsible

* Letter to Mr Pitt, p. 20. 2d *edit*.
† p. 216, &c.

funds, it is apt to be shaken by that consternation which is apt to spread, after a succession of commercial bankruptcies, or during the alarms of war. At such a period, it has been particularly found, that the notes of country banks, which chiefly circulate among consumers and petty dealers, have fallen into distrust with that large portion of the people. If one bank should fail, a run upon all those in the neighbourhood immediately takes place, and diffuses general distress. Such of the country bankers, as are most prudent, adopt a preventive caution, by limiting, of their own accord, the issue of their notes; and all of them are forced to enlarge that fund of cash, with which they may be prepared to answer demands. In consequence of these operations, an additional quantity of gold and of Bank of England notes must be carried down from London into the country, both to supply that void in the channel of circulation from which the discredited country notes have been thrown out, and to form that additional reserve which the bankers must keep in their coffers. But the money-dealers and traders of the capital will, in some degree, participate that consternation to which the whole country has given way: it will appear to them also a necessary precaution, that they should enlarge their fund against contingencies, and keep a larger supply of Bank of England notes than they find necessary in ordinary times. By these multiplied hoards, as well as by the quantity of cash sent into the country, the circulating money of the metropolis must suffer a very great diminution. But it was previously no more than sufficient to effect the necessary payments; and on the punctual discharge of these, the whole commercial credit of the kingdom depends. Unless the Bank of England, therefore, which is the source of circulating medium, shall, in these circumstances, consent to enlarge its issue of paper, a general subversion and ruin of that credit may take place; but if it adopts such a measure seasonably, and in the proportion which the new demands of the circulation require, the mischief may cease after a slight and temporary inconvenience. Beside this remedial policy, which can only be adopted after the evil has been felt to some extent, that body, in order to be prepared against such an event, ought to keep at all times in its treasury such an additional quantity of gold, as may be sufficient to meet this extraordinary demand, and to supply the place of those country notes that are liable to be extinguished. But although such appears to be the real policy of that institution, we can scarcely be surprised if it has not always very clearly understood it to be so, and has sometimes evinced a reluctance to pursue this line of conduct. The task of supplying gold to all the country banks, under the expense with which the collection of it is frequently attended, may be considered indeed as imposed upon the Bank of England by that monopoly, which compensates this hardship by other advantages. But to enlarge the issue of their paper, at the very time that their fund of gold is diminishing, is a measure, which would confessedly be imprudent in every inferior establishment, and which on that account the directors of the great bank have not always perceived that they were warranted, by the peculiarity of their situation, to adopt, as the real means of checking the drain of their gold. Some of the circumstances, which distinguished the memorable year 1793, illustrate at once the soundness of the policy which is here described, and the very recent period at which the bank still showed itself insufficiently aware of it. In the distress of that year, the Bank of England was unwilling to extend its aid to the country banks, or to augment the issue of its own paper. Several opulent houses, that applied for assistance, were refused discounts, because they did not offer London securities; but the important failures, which immediately ensued, proved that the relief of the country was necessary to the solvency of the metropolis. The pressure originated in an extraordinary demand for guineas in the country; but the want of bank notes in London soon became the principal evil. The notes, previously in circulation, were not below the usual number; but that was rendered, by a slower circulation, insufficient for the necessary payments. As the Bank of England did not think proper to enlarge the quantity of its paper, a remedy of exactly the same kind was administered by Parliament. A loan of Exchequer bills was directed to be made, to as many mercantile persons, giving proper security, as should apply; and it is a most interesting fact, that credit began to recover itself some time before those bills were actually delivered. The very expectation of this supply of an article, which almost any trader might obtain, and then convert it into bank notes and guineas, diffused an idea of general solvency. The punctuality of the London payments being restored, the distress of the whole country was gradually removed. Of the five millions, which the Exchequer had been authorized by Parliament to advance, not one half was taken, and no part was lost; on the contrary, a profit resulted to Government, from the small compensation of additional interest, which was paid by the borrowers. This seasonable measure was not understood at the time, and was opposed on some grounds of constitutional jealousy; but the result of its operation has cast a steady light on our actual system of circulation, and on the true policy of the national bank. In future seasons of alarm, it may reasonably be expected, that the directors of that body will prove less timid; as it is to be

48

hoped, that experience has taught the country banks to enlarge their usual provision of convertible funds.*

The most serious danger, to which the Bank of England itself is exposed, is that of being drained of its specie. It may be subjected to such a drain, as is intimated in the preceding observations, in consequence of that alarm which occasions a great demand for guineas, either to be hoarded, or to supply the place of paper thrown out of circulation. Indeed, if the alarm is of long continuance, and the Bank maintains in circulation no more than its usual quantity of notes, it may be altogether exhausted of its guineas, however small that quantity of notes may be; because if these are always re-issued in loans upon the discount of bills, they may be perpetually returned upon the Bank in demand for more specie. Let the alarm be great enough, and of sufficient duration; and the Bank, by maintaining only a million of notes in circulation, may, by the continual return of these, be exhausted of fifty millions of guineas. But, in general, a more permanent cause of a run upon the Bank of England for specie, is the excess of the market price of gold above its mint price. In former times, this was occasioned by the debased state of gold currency; and the Bank was obliged to submit to the accumulated and provoking expense of coining new guineas, which were immediately melted down, that the bullion might be sold to the Bank itself at the high market price. Since the gold currency was reformed, a temporary excess of the market price of gold above its mint price, has been produced by a temporary disadvantage in the balance of foreign trade; that having been occasioned sometimes by the large importations of grain after a deficient harvest, and more frequently by unproductive exportations to defray the expenses of war, or the subsidies to foreign allies. In whatever manner the high price of gold is produced, immediate demands are made upon the Bank for guineas, in order to export them. These it endeavours to replace, though gold cannot be purchased without a considerable loss. A most unequal competition will thus be established, between the Bank, on the one hand, which buys and coins at a great loss, and the clandestine dealers, on the other hand, who melt and sell at a great profit. It will no longer be necessary for the latter to export more gold, than what is above the immediate demand of the Bank: the operation will now be confined to London; the melters and coiners living upon the same spot, and affording constant employment to each other. If the unfavourable balance of trade, which has caused this high price of bullion, were not of a temporary nature, the Bank of England, by this continued accumulation of

* Pp. 49. 71–96. 172–187.

49

unproductive expense, might ultimately be reduced to very great distress. And if an unfavourable balance, originating in the expenses of foreign warfare or alliance, should at any time be loaded with the additional payments of a larger importation of grain, while the embarrassments of the national Bank were still farther aggravated by domestic alarm and a general disorder of mercantile credit; under such a combination of inauspicious circumstances, the usual means of prudence and the rules of ordinary policy might be expected to fail, and necessity would be left to justify those desperate measures which it might suggest.*

But this excess of the market price of gold above its mint price, may likewise be produced, as we formerly explained, by too great a quantity of paper-money. The Bank indeed, as it has also been shown, has the power of restricting the country paper, by limiting its own notes to those which are actually needed for the purposes of circulation. It has, therefore, the power in a great degree of preventing that high price of gold, and the consequent drain of its own guineas, which proceed from an excessive circulation of paper. So long as the Bank is liable to payments in specie, it has thus an evident interest to prevent its own paper, as well as that of the whole country, from being so excessive, as to occasion a rise in the price of commodities. To understand this clearly, and to attend carefully to its operation, forms a very important branch of the policy of the Bank of England. As its notes are issued in loans to the merchants, it can only limit the extent of that issue, by restricting the amount of the loans. Hence it appears, that the Bank ought to regulate the total amount of its loans, with a view to the quantity of circulating medium, independent altogether of the solvency and opulence of those who wish to become borrowers, and of the character of the bills that are offered for discount. There may be a disposition among very rich traders, to borrow a sum far exceeding what it would be proper for the Bank to lend, although it entertained no doubt of punctual repayment. But, by the laws that confine the rate of interest, and which still remain in force after every competent judge has been long convinced of their uselessness and inconvenience, the Bank of England is deprived of the most natural and simple means of restricting the amount of its loans. It is prohibited, even in time of war, from demanding an interest of more than five *per cent.*, which is the rate at which it discounts during peace. This has generally been found sufficient, during peace, to limit the demand upon the Bank for loans; because mercantile profits are then low, from the abundance of capital, and the activity of competition. The applications for

* Pp. 90. 115–153.

discounts have often, during such a period, fallen short of what the Bank was really disposed to afford. But in time of war, the rate of mercantile profit, from the scarcity of capital, is extremely high. There is an irresistible temptation, therefore, to borrow from the Bank at a cheap rate, that the great profits may be gained upon a commercial employment of the money. Accordingly, in time of war, and especially during the last years of it, the directors have often been subjected to very earnest and clamorous solicitations for discount. Were they permitted to raise their rate of interest, it would follow that of mercantile profit, and the demand upon the Bank for loans, would at all times be accompanied by an effectual principle of limitation. But under the existing prohibitions of law, the directors are forced to have recourse to the expedient of specifying, according to their discretion, the total sum which they will at any one time venture to lend to the merchants. According to a recent determination of their court, this sum is specified weekly, in order that they may have a frequent opportunity of varying it, according to the fluctuation of circumstances.*

To limit the total amount of paper issued, and to resort, whenever the temptation of borrowing is strong, to some effectual principle of restriction; never to diminish greatly the sum in circulation, but to let it vibrate only within certain limits: to afford a slow and cautious extension of it, as the general trade of the country is enlarged; and to permit a temporary increase during an extraordinary period of difficulty or alarm: this, in the language of Mr Thornton, is the true policy of the directors of an institution, placed in the circumstances of the Bank of England.†

We have thus collected, from various passages of Mr Thornton's discourse, the general lineaments of that system of credit and circulation, which is at present established; refraining from the insertion of any criticisms that might have interrupted the description. Some parts of his account are not sufficiently dilated, to convey precise information; and others, in which some reasoning is implicated with the statements of fact, cannot be admitted without hesitation. But we are not confident enough in our knowledge of the subject, to enter into these minute corrections. One general remark, however, which was strongly impressed upon ourselves by the facts of the preceding narrative, we cannot forbear to express, although it does not lie within the scope of Mr Thornton's discussions. If the Bank of England must now be considered as a national establishment, not merely influencing, by the superior magnitude of its capital, the state of commercial circulation, but

* Pp. 147. 246. 283.
† P. 295.

51

guiding its movements according to views of public policy, an important revolution has taken place since the first erection of that corporation as a banking establishment. That power of issuing the medium of exchange, with the opportunities it implies of varying its quantity and value, which, while precious coin was in use, was exercised under the immediate prerogative of the Crown, is now virtually invested in the Governor and Directors of the Bank of England. In the official character of that Board, some of the functions of sovereignty are united to those of a trader; and the opportunities of banking profits are blended with a trust and charge of the public interest. It will be pleasing, if these shall prove more happily compatible, than they have been found in other instances. The organization of this establishment, possessed of such means to control the operations of commerce, as well as to facilitate the advance of financial supplies, may, into our political constitution already so complicated, introduce a new principle of action, the effect of which cannot be clearly discerned. Perhaps, an unbounded field will be opened for the extension of ministerial influence. Perhaps, an unexpected control may be gained to the people, over the views and measures of the executive.

III. In the foregoing view of the dangers to which the Bank is occasionally exposed, our readers must have already perceived the account which Mr Thornton gives of the embarrassments, that led to the memorable order of Council in February 1797. The suspension of cash payments was an event, in his opinion, to which the national Bank was liable from its very nature; the probability of which has been too studiously concealed; and to the recurrence of which we may look forward.* The gold, in the coffers of the Bank, had been much reduced by the effect of an unfavourable balance of trade. The alarms of invasion had led to the failure of some country banks in the North of England; this occasioned a farther demand for guineas from the Bank, and a diminution in the circulating notes of London. The Directors aggravated the distress, and augmented the demand for guineas, by un-advisedly suppressing some of their notes, instead of enlarging the quantity.†

We cannot entertain a doubt, that these were the principal causes of embarrassment; but that other circumstances at the same time co-operated, which Mr Thornton has rather too anxiously avoided to mention. Under the unfavourable balance of trade, which he notices by this general expression, we must include the effect of foreign subsidies. And we suspect that that

* Pp. 146. 247.
† Pp. 72. 95.

52

diminution in the quantity of notes, which the merchants could command, was not altogether owing to an ignorance, on the part of the Directors, of the proper remedy for the existing evil. Mr Thornton indeed employs several elaborate pages,* to relieve the Bank from every degree of blame, on account of its loans to Government. But this appears quite ineffectual against the evidence which was laid before Parliament, of the sentiments which the Directors themselves entertained. In various resolutions of their Court, and in letters to the Chancellor of the Exchequer, they stated the serious apprehensions, as well as the actual embarrassment, which they felt from their unprecedented advances on Treasury bills; and, in their memorial to the Cabinet, they described it as an unconstitutional mode of raising money, to which they were not warranted by their charter to consent. After this, it is vain for any advocate of the Bank, now to maintain, that those loans were altogether free from imprudence or culpability. At the same time we are ready to acknowledge, what was not very distinctly perceived in the first discussions of this event, that the loans to Government had no *direct* tendency to produce the particular distress, which was relieved by the restriction of payments. That consisted, unquestionably, in the progressive drain of specie; which those loans neither occasioned nor increased, because they were paid into the Exchequer in notes. This run upon the Bank for specie, was chiefly occasioned by the deficient quantity of money in circulation; which the advances to Government, in their direct operation, rather contributed to repair, because the notes were of course issued from the Exchequer almost immediately into the market. But at the same time it must be remarked, though Mr Thornton seems studiously to have kept this out of view, that, by their indirect and unavoidable operation, these loans of the Bank to Government contributed to aggravate that distress of the circulation, which was mainly produced by other causes. For some time prior to the suspension of payments, the Bank of England had limited its discount of commercial paper. To this hurtful measure it was undoubtedly obliged to have recourse, in consequence of having granted a much greater accommodation to Government than it was warranted to give, which imposed the prudential necessity of giving less accommodation to the merchants than it had been accustomed to afford. Such a diminution of discounts could not occur at any period, without producing a certain degree of mercantile distress, both by the disappointment of payments actually promised, and by interrupting the usual course of pecuniary arrangements. But at that

* Pp. 96–111.

53

particular juncture, a great distress already subsisted, which the conduct of the Bank towards the merchants had a necessary tendency to aggravate. A similar diminution of the Bank discounts, by narrowing the facilities of credit, would at any time render the existing quantity of circulating medium less adequate, than before, to the necessities of the market. At that particular juncture, money was already deficient, from the operation of other causes; and became still more inadequate to its necessary purposes, when a restriction of credit took place, which both rendered a greater quantity of money requisite to drive the same trade, and retarded the circulation of that already in the market. While we agree with Mr Thornton, therefore, that the loans to Government could not tend to diminish the sum of notes in circulation; we must contend against him, that they did tend to distress the circulation, by rendering that sum of notes less adequate to the wants of commerce, than if they had flowed into the market through the usual channel of discounts. He asserts, on the contrary, that 'it is the total quantity of circulating notes, and not the manner in which they come into circulation, that is the material point:' but nothing can be more unsatisfactory and cumbrous, than the illustrations by which he labours to expound this very fallacious position. It is indeed inconsistent with the fundamental principles, which are elucidated by all the reasonings and tenor of his book.

The suspension of payments in specie was properly continued, according to Mr Thornton, from the permanence of those circumstances which rendered it originally necessary: an unfavourable exchange, produced partly by our heavy expenditures, but chiefly aggravated by vast importations of corn; and the prevalence, till the eve of peace, of alarms about hostile invasions.* It is not altogether superfluous to remark, that the restriction of payments, until after the cessation of hostilities, was provided for by law, long before those deficient harvests had been felt, to which so great a portion of this necessity is ascribed. And the continuance of the suspension was officially justified in Parliament, upon the alleged, but not very intelligible, ground of resisting certain designs of the enemy to ruin our public credit. The whole circumstances of the measure, both in the first event and in its subsequent renewal, in the arguments that were publicly urged to prove its necessity, and in the explanation which Mr Thornton has given of its nature, conspire to prove that it originated in the direct consequences of the war itself; although this view of the subject was most earnestly discountenanced at the time.

* P. 143.

IV. In the first part of our abstract, we explained Mr Thornton's opinion, that an extravagant issue of paper will raise the price of commodities, and depreciate the currency in its bullion value. He has therefore admitted the general principles, from which Mr Boyd and others have inferred that the Bank of England has, within the last few years, issued an excessive quantity of paper. Against the validity of that inference, however, he contends that, in point of fact, the Bank of England has not extended the number of its notes, since the suspension of its cash payments; and that the rise of prices and depreciation of currency, from which that enlargement has been presumed, may arise from other causes. Among such causes, he mentions the necessary influence of war, of accumulated taxes, and of a scarcity continued for two years, in raising the price of all commodities; and the effect of an immense importation of corn in turning the exchange against us, and thus raising the market price of gold. That all of these circumstances have cooperated in raising prices, we have no doubt; but we are by no means satisfied that they are adequate to explain the whole effect. War, it must be observed, and taxes, and a scarcity of provisions in its direct operation, increase the real or bullion price of goods, and have no tendency to produce an excess of the market above the mint price of gold. The importation of grain, by turning the balance of trade against us, does tend to produce that excess; but the excess, which we have lately witnessed, has been perhaps both too great and too permanent to be explained wholly in this manner. We doubt extremely, if it could have been produced without that depreciation of our currency, which originates in excessive quantity.

Mr Thornton, however, has endeavoured to show*, that the circulating paper of the Bank of England does not in fact amount now to a greater sum than, upon an average of years, was in circulation before the suspension of cash payments. Upon an average of three years, ending in December 1795, their amount, according to the evidence laid before Parliament, was 11,975,573*l.* By a subsequent statement presented to the House of Commons, they amounted in December 1800, to 15,450,970*l.* From the difference between these two sums, however, Mr Thornton insists that we ought to deduct the amount of two millions, consisting of one and two pound notes, which have displaced, he alleges, in the circulation, an equal sum of guineas. After this deduction, there still remains the sum of 1,475,397*l.*, by which the Bank paper exceeded, in 1800, its average amount before the suspension of cash payments. But in the spring of 1801, the Governor of the

* P. 225.

55

Bank stated to the House of Commons, that the Company had reduced its notes to a sum less, by about a million and a half, than their amount in the preceding December. Whether this evidence, under all the assumptions which it involves, may be considered as completely satisfactory, in opposition to the presumptions that are warranted by the general argument, we shall not venture to pronounce. We may suggest, however, to our readers, the propriety of adding to the foregoing statement, a fact of which we are apprised by Mr Thornton,* that the enumeration of *country banks* taken in 1800, differed from that taken in 1797, by the excess of 386 above 353. And to those who recollect that Mr Boyd's pamphlet was published on 31st December 1800, it will not fail to occur as a circumstance which that gentleman might plausibly urge as a confirmation of his reasonings, that in the course of the three months immediately ensuing, the Bank thought it expedient to call in a million and a half of its notes.

We have expressed ourselves with unaffected doubt, with regard to this alleged dependence of the present rate of prices on the present state of paper currency, because it appears to us a problem, of which a satisfactory solution has not yet been offered. According to that view of the question, indeed, which seems to us the most correct as well as the most simple, a sufficient answer will be assigned, if the excess of the market price of gold above its mint price shall be found to continue, notwithstanding the permanent restoration of the balance of trade to its accustomed preponderancy in our favour. In the mean time, we should be glad to see the fact itself, of which the origin and cause are thus anxiously sought, perspicuously stated under its most necessary distinctions and limitations. It may perhaps be in the power of those, who have paid attention to such minute but valuable details, to date the first appearances of this recent increase of prices, and to trace its progressive diffusion over all the relations of internal exchange. In such a statement, it would be necessary, likewise, to specify in what proportion this rise is locally confined to our own island, or common to us with the Continent of Europe; and to distinguish in what proportion that local rise consists of a real increase in the bullion price, and of a nominal increase only in the currency price.

* P. 155.

Vol. I ([No. II] Jan. 1803), Art. XVI (pp. 431–450).
Principes d'Economie Politiqae, ouvrage couronné par l'Institut National, dans sa Séance du 15 Nivose, an IX; et depuis revu, corrigé et augmenté par l'Auteur. Par N. F. Canard, Ancien Professeur de Mathématiques à l'Ecole Centrale de Moulins. Paris, 1801. 8vo.

IN the year 1800, the National Institute of France proposed the following question, as a subject of prize essays: '*Is it true, that, in an agricultural country, taxes of every description fall ultimately on the proprietors of land?*' The problem is highly important, but of very difficult solution. It has attracted the attention of economical authors, both in England and upon the Continent, for more than a century; though, prior to the speculations of Quesnai, it can hardly be said to have ever been stated in a very strict form. Since the first publication of that philosopher's discoveries, his famous project of a territorial tax has been the subject of much reasoning among French writers; whose topics on both sides were so plausible, that the argument was not yet brought to a close, when the distractions of the Revolution suspended for a while the calm discussions of philosophy. It is pleasing to observe, after the tempest has subsided, that the minds of men spring back to the same difficulties which formerly provoked their emulation, and exercised their ingenuity. Amidst, indeed, that undistinguishing reprobation of the past, which in the feelings of the populace has very naturally succeeded to fanaticism and terror, the Economists are confounded with the Jacobins and Anarchists; the enlightened advocates of regulated freedom have been classed with the most criminal disturbers of social peace. But though the name of those virtuous sages is for a while subjected to unjust calumny, and though their excellent writings may be laid aside or prohibited, the impulse which they gave to the public mind still remains in force. The important questions which they started, again occur for investigation. The reforms of administration, which they recommended, force themselves upon the memory of those who have witnessed a change of dynasty, rather than of system. Even those prospects of political improvement, which flattered the benevolent anticipations of the economists, will soon be recognized as sound conclusions of science; and it will at length be acknowledged that Turgot, and Mirabeau, and Quesnai, were the friends of mankind, and that their genius and their labours were devoted to the refinement of social happiness, and the consolidation of the political fabric.

57

The prize of the National Institute was adjudged to M. Canard for a memoir, which, by subsequent alterations, he has formed into the present work. It certainly does not present a satisfactory solution of the question proposed, nor even, in our opinion, an approximation to it; on the contrary, we are inclined to suspect, that the view which he has taken of the subject is in many respects erroneous. His Essay, however, is written with considerable ability. From some of the following criticisms, it will probably appear, that he has added nothing to our knowledge of political economy, and that the style and form which he has adopted, are not very well calculated either to illustrate or to diffuse truths already ascertained. At the same time, the work will be read with pleasure by those, who, being already masters of the subject, can be gratified with the variety of aspects under which it may be considered, as well as with the comparative state of their favourite science among the learned of different countries.

In conducting his investigation of the problem proposed by the Institute, the author found himself obliged to recur to some of the fundamental principles in the theory of political economy. The truth is, that the equable diffusion, or exclusive incidence of taxes, cannot be ascertained by any direct induction of particular facts; but must be obtained synthetically, after a just analysis, both of price and of the order according to which the annual produce is distributed among the people. M. Canard has therefore given his Essay a more general title than belongs to the question which first suggested it; and he appears, by this title, to have been tempted to introduce several chapters which have no relation to the principal object of inquiry.

In the *first* chapter, the author gives an explanation of fundamental principles; or rather of the sense in which he employs certain terms: for they are stated more in the manner of definitions that are assumed, than of truths to which we are conducted by analysis. He begins with illustrating a distinction between necessary and superfluous labour: by the former, he means that of which the produce is indispensably necessary to the existence and preservation of man, as well as to the continuance or replacement of stock: by the latter, he means that portion which ministers to our superfluous accommodations, and of which the produce, if not consumed in superfluous enjoyment, goes to augment the quantity of accumulated stock. He afterwards proceeds to this position, that every thing which has exchangeable value derives its price from the several quantities of labour that have successively been employed upon it. As different forms of the same proposition, he assumes, that all property consists in so much accumulated

58

labour; and that the exchangeable value of every portion of property consists in the labour which it will purchase or command. What other writers, accordingly, have called accumulated stock or capital, he denominates *travail exigible*; and as every addition to this accumulated stock is derived from the produce of what he has styled superfluous labour, he introduces another epithet into this phrase, denominating accumulated stock *travail superflu exigible*. Proceeding in the application of these terms, he asserts, that all wealth, property, and riches, consist only of *travail superflu exigible*; and that necessary labour, being absorbed either in necessary consumption, or in the replacement of capital, can never form a part of the actual mass of riches. In the same style, he lays it down as a principle, that it is the accumulation of unconsumed superfluous labour, which creates all the sources of revenue; from which it follows, that all revenue consists in the profit of this accumulated stock.

In all this, M. Canard appears to us to display very little sagacity. He has, without any necessity, affected to change the established forms of expression; and has confounded principles which are very carefully distinguished in the works from which he evidently derived his information. In asserting that exchangeable value consists of labour stored up, he appears to have preferred the errors of our English writers to the accurate and precise notions of exchangeable value which he might have found in various excellent works, published in his own language; particularly those of M. Turgot and of the Abbé Morellet. But we shall, in another part of this article, enter into a more detailed explanation of the fallacies involved in this supposition. It appears quite a puerile mistake to say, that accumulated stock alone is wealth; and that the produce, reserved for immediate consumption, forms no portion of the mass of riches. Surely, it is the capability of being consumed, that renders any produce a part of wealth; and if it were necessary to make a distinction, in this respect, between stock already in consumption, and stock accumulated into capital, it would be more natural and more just to say, that the latter indirectly aids the production of riches, while the former itself is wealth. It suggests also a very imperfect view of the subject to say, that accumulated wealth is the *source* of all revenue. It is unquestionably a necessary condition for the reproduction of revenue; but it is only one of several conditions, all of which are necessary. In the theory of national wealth, the natural fertility of the soil, the natural powers of human labour, and the accumulation of capital for the requisite advances, are all of them conditions of which the existence is indispensable to reproduction. It gives

59

but a partial view of the actual arrangements of nature, to fix upon any one of them, singly, as the source of revenue: yet such is the propensity of speculative men to simplify, that each of the three conditions has been separated from the rest for that purpose. The economists selected the first; some other French writers, who have not risen to such reputation, insist upon the second; and M. Canard, with less plausibility than either, has affirmed that the source of revenue is accumulated stock. It was an unavoidable corollary from that proposition, to infer, as he has done, that all revenue consists in the profit of stock. But he loses, in this manner, the advantages of that very useful and accurate classification, which distinguishes revenue, according to the three great orders of the people among whom it is distributed, into rent, profit, and wages.

The *second* chapter, on *Money*, is a very trivial one. It contains nothing but what the author might have assumed as familiar to all his readers. The work is certainly not suited to those to whom the subject is entirely new. But this chapter does not even enumerate one half of the propositions, with regard to money, which may now be considered as perfectly well ascertained.

The subject of the *third* chapter is the *determination of the price of commodities*. It opens with a very formal and distinct enunciation of the principle, which we have already noticed in our account of the first, and which assigns the quantity of labour employed on a commodity, as the essential constituent and measure of its exchangeable value. This notion, which is certainly incorrect, is far from being peculiar to M. Canard: it is much employed in the treatise of Smith on the Wealth of Nations, and has the effect of involving, in very great obscurity, all the observations which that profound author has delivered on the analysis of price. An ingenious and very learned economist* appears to have supposed, that this principle originated with Mr Rice Vaughan, whose excellent discourse on coinage was composed during the reign of Charles I.; but it may be found in writers of a much earlier date, and, to omit the intermediate authorities, is expressly stated and illustrated in a passage of Aristotle's Ethics.† There is, indeed, no necessity of supposing, that any one of these writers borrowed the idea from his predecessors: it is one of those errors which are obviously suggested by our uncorrected notions of natural equity. As it has been admitted without suspicion, into some systematical works which deservedly possess a high reputation, and still continue to infect the reasonings of many politicians, our readers, we

* Plan for altering the manner of collecting a large portion of the public revenue, &c. By the Earl of Lauderdale.
† Ethic. Nichom. V. c. 8. Edit. Duval.

hope, will not be displeased that we take this opportunity of explaining our reasons for rejecting it. It is proper that we should transcribe M. Canard's statement in his own language.

'Il s'agit maintenant de déterminer ce qui fixe le prix de ce qui a de la valeur parmi les hommes. D'abord, le prix n'est autre chose que le rapport de valeur d'une chose à une autre; et comme on compare tout à la valeur de l'or ou de l'argent, le prix est le rapport de la valeur de chaque chose à celle d'une quantité déterminée de l'un ou de l'autre de ces métaux. Or, maintenant, quelle est la cause que peuvent déterminer ces différens rapports; ou, ce qui revient au même, quel est le principe qui assigne à chaque chose sa valeur? Il est certain d'abord que, puisque tout ce qui a du prix est le résultat du travail, la valeur d'un objet quelconque doit être en raison du travail qu'il a coûté. Il est certain, en second lieu, que, si tous les hommes étaient bornés aux besoins absolus de leur conservation, si tout leur travail était naturel, et qu'il ne différât que par le temps, ce serait la durée seule du travail qui en mesurerait la valeur: ainsi les jours et les heures seraient les unités et les fractions d'unités nominales qui détermineraient les valeurs de toutes choses. C'est probablement à de semblables divisions de temps que doivent leur première origine les unités nominales adoptées chez les différens peuples, telles que le franc, la livre sterling, le florin, etc. Mais les différentes espèces de travail appris présentent une si grande variété dans la valeur du travail, que le temps ne peut lui servir de mesure.' p. 26. 27.

When labour is said to be a measure of exchangeable value, there are two senses in which this proposition may be understood; two ways in which the labour, that is to form this measure, may be estimated. The exchangeable value of a commodity may either be measured by the quantity of labour that had been employed in its own production, or by the labour that had been employed on the commodity for which it is exchanged. According to the doctrine which we are about to examine, these two quantities of labour must have been equal. Those authors, accordingly, who urge this doctrine most confidently, use, as their measure of value, sometimes the one quantity, and sometimes the other. That the value or price of an article depends on the labour that has been employed in producing it, and that the value or price of an article consists in the labour which it will purchase or command, are stated by them as the same proposition in two forms.

Though it were true, in point of fact, that what is given in exchange for a commodity is just so much labour as was employed in producing the other commodity for which it is exchanged, it would be a nugatory inference, that that labour measures the exchangeable value of the first commodity. The conclusion would

61

reach no farther than this, that, in the exchange of two subjects, each measures the exchangeable value of the other; or that the exchangeable value of a certain quantity of any one article, may be measured by the quantity of another for which it is actually exchanged. But, in point of fact, it is not true that the thing purchased in every bargain is merely so much labour; for the value of the raw material, on which that has been employed, can neither, to use the language of mathematicians, be rejected as nothing, nor estimated as a constant quantity. The value of raw materials, like that of manufactured articles, and of labour itself, varies with the proportion of supply and demand. In some manufactures, indeed, the price of the raw material is, in proportion to the labour employed, almost infinitely small: for example, the value of the flax in a pair of lace ruffles, that of the kelp and sand in a vessel of cut glass, that of the iron and charcoal in a steel watch-spring. But, in all these instances, the supply of the raw material is abundant. There are other manufactures, in which the value of the raw material is, in proportion to that of the labour employed, by no means so small. In a shawl of Cashmere, for example, the value of the wool, which is of a very rare kind, greatly exceeds the value of all the labour bestowed in weaving and embroidering it. In the price of a diamond, the whole value of the labour employed by the miner, the lapidary, and the jeweller, may be considered as almost infinitely small in comparison of the value of that labour, if we may use the expression, which Nature has bestowed in effecting such a beautiful and rare crystallization of one of her most ordinary substances.

It is equally incorrect to say, that the exchangeable value of a commodity may be measured, or is determined, by the labour that has been employed in its production. That the wages of the whole labour, employed in production or in manufacture, form a component part of price, is an undeniable principle; in other words, that the quantity of the commodity bought must be adequate to replace, by a circuit of other exchanges, the whole commodities advanced or consumed in the manufacture of the commodity sold. But the proper mode of introducing this principle into the theory of exchangeable value, is, not to state the value of labour as constituting the whole price, or forming an adequate measure of it, but to view it as a condition which limits the eventual supply of each commodity. If the whole quantity of commodities, advanced or consumed in the production of an article, be not replaced by its exchangeable value in the market, the supply of that particular commodity will certainly be so far lessened, until, by the influence of this diminution upon its value, that replacement is complete.

But, in the actual exchange of any one commodity for any other, no regard is paid to the quantity of labour employed in producing either; the quantities, reciprocally exchanged, are proportioned by the competition between the supply and demand of both. These are subject to continual fluctuation. If of two commodities, the demand of the one is increasing at a particular time while the supply remains unaugmented, and the demand of the other is diminishing while the supply remains undiminished, it is manifest, that, at that particular time, the respective quantities of the two commodities exchanged for each other may have cost, in their production, very unequal quantities of labour. Quantities of labour, it is probable, very nearly equal, are expended, in order to send to the London market the finest black and the finest blue cloths. But a sudden death in the royal family will raise the price of black cloth to the height of twice or thrice that of blue; one yard of the former will be considered as exchanging for two or three yards of the latter; that is, in the language of which we dispute the propriety, a certain quantity of labour is given on the one side, for twice or thrice that quantity of labour on the other.

It is evident, that all the errors on which we have animadverted, originate in an imperfect view of the real nature of exchangeable value, and of the principle by which it is at all times regulated. We shall therefore take this opportunity of stating and explaining its definition.

The value of any commodity is the assignable quantity of any other commodity, for which an assigned quantity of the former may be exchanged. In this respect, every commodity may be considered as exchangeable for every other; and what we call the value of any one, may be expressed by assigning a quantity of any other. Under the name of commodities, in this general definition, we comprehend not only rude produce, and manufactured articles of every kind, but money, likewise, or the coined metals of every denomination, and labour of every description.

The reciprocal value of any two commodities, that is, the respective portions of each, which are exchanged for one another, is determined in every instance of exchange by competition; or by the proportion between the supply and the demand of each of the two commodities. The exchangeable value, therefore, of any two commodities is liable to vary with the variation of four circumstances, and will depend upon the result of the combined variations of all. These four circumstances are, the demand and the supply of the one commodity, and the demand and supply of the other. Whoever attempts to ascertain the variation of prices from one age to another, must, with respect to every two commodities

63

compared together, take into consideration all of these four circumstances. There can be no doubt, that the exchangeable value of labour, that is, the quantity of corn or of cloth, for example, which is given in exchange for a certain quantity of labour, is regulated at all times by the result of the same four circumstances: the supply of that particular species of labour which is in question, —the demand for that particular labour,—the supply of the particular kind of grain or cloth in question,—and the demand for that grain, or that cloth. All of these circumstances severally affect the reciprocal value of any one kind of labour as exchanged for any one kind of grain, or for any one kind of cloth. Let us take for an example, the labour of a common ploughman, and estimate the exchangeable value of that quantity which is understood to be included in a day's work, in terms of one particular species of grain, such as oats. It is evident that the quantity of oats given in exchange for a day's labour at the plough, will become greater, if there is either a diminished supply of ploughmen, or an increased demand for them,—or an increased supply of oats, or a diminished demand for that sort of grain. On the other hand, the quantity of oats, given in exchange for a day's labour at the plough, will become less, if there is either an increased supply of ploughmen, or a diminished demand for them,—or a diminished supply of oats, or an increased demand for that sort of grain. In each of these single changes, while the three other circumstances remain permanent, the change of relative price will take place as already described. But two, or more, or all, of the four circumstances may be fluctuating at one time; and the final result of value will depend upon the degree in which the several variations cooperate, or counteract the effect of each other.

Though M. Canard has adopted, in its most unqualified form, the error which we have thus endeavoured to expose, it has not led him to any false conclusions in his account of the manner in which prices are determined. He appears to have contented himself with establishing it absolutely, as an important and fundamental truth in political economy; and, with an inconsistency, of which he seems unaware, proceeds to derive from the principle of mutual competition the various conclusions which he has arranged, in this fifth chapter, on the subject of prices. It may be inferred, from the details into which we have found it necessary to enter, that he has not stated that principle in the most explicit manner, nor developed all the consequences, with respect to the theory of exchange, which it involves. The style, likewise, in which he has presented the subject, is liable to great objection. He has thought proper to adopt the language and forms of algebra; and several pages, and even folded sheets, are crowded with characters and symbols. It is right that our readers should have a specimen of this, as well as of the other parts of the work. Let the difference between the highest price demanded by the sellers, and the lowest price offered by the buyers, be called L; and let x represent that part of this difference which the sellers are finally content to take in addition to the lowest price; $L - x$ will be that other portion of the difference, which the buyers finally succeed in retrenching from the highest price. Call the desire of the buyers to purchase B, and their competition N; call the desire of the sellers to dispose of their goods b, and their competition n. It is evident that x, the portion of the difference that is paid by the buyers, will increase in proportion to their desire and their competition; x will therefore be in the ratio compounded of B and of N, or will increase as BN. For the same reason, the other portion $L - x$ will increase as bn. We have thus the following proportion, $x : BN : : L - x : bn$, which gives the equation, $bnx = BN(L - x)$, from which we get $x = \dfrac{BN}{BN + bn} L$. He proceeds through twenty pages with this calculation, into which a great many more terms, as well as new symbols, are introduced: But our readers, we conceive, have already had enough of it.

In its own province, the peculiar language of algebra will never fail to gratify those who can appreciate the admirable structure of the most perfect instrument that has yet been invented by man. But that injudicious and unskilful pedantry ought most severely to be censured, which diverts an instrument from its proper use, and attempts to remove those landmarks by which the sciences are bounded from each other. The peculiar forms of expression, which have been introduced into the modern analysis, are sanctioned by the facilities which they afford, both of perspicuous abridgement, and of prosecuting a train of investigation to new and remote results. But M. Canard has only translated, into a language less readily understood, truths, of which the ordinary enunciation is intelligible and familiar to all. We will not deny that some branches of political economy, especially those which relate to circulation, money, and the analysis of price, admit of being treated with a precision, which almost approaches to mathematical exactness. But a subject may possess this precision, without requiring, or even admitting, the symbolic representations of algebra. We would not even exclude altogether the use of analogies borrowed from mathematical learning: they afford much delight to those minds which are habituated to pass occasionally from the vague conclusions of moral induction to the full assurance

65

of knowledge in the stricter sciences. Both as illustrations, and as ornaments, such analogies may be introduced with the happiest effect. But the frugal and classic taste, with which Beccaria has interspersed allusions of this nature, forms a contrast to the pedantry and profusion with which M. Canard has overloaded his composition.

The *fourth* chapter treats *of the circulation of money and of credit.* It contains a tolerably correct view of the leading propositions upon that subject; but none of them are presented in a new light, or traced to any new consequences.

In the *fifth* chapter, which is entitled, *on the causes of the increase and the decline of wealth,* he professes to demonstrate, that the prosperity of states has a necessary limit; that industry and economy must ultimately give place to luxurious and wasteful expense; and that nations are destined, by a law of nature, to fluctuate in a series of changes. The opinion is far from being new; he has placed it, however, in a new aspect. The reverses, which are exhibited by the history of the most celebrated states, have suggested this melancholy idea, and, in so early an age of the world as the present, they still give it too much plausibility: yet, it may be doubted, if it be not more agreeable to the just rules of philosophical anticipation, to flatter ourselves with a prospect of unchecked improvements in opulence as in knowledge, than to acquiesce in that mournful analogy which assimilates the political fortunes of a people to the progress of individual life, and subjects to the same law of necessary alternation, the geological surface of our planet, and the prosperity of its diversified inhabitants. Whichsoever of these conclusions may ultimately be verified, one thing at present seems probable, that a just statement of the moral and political destinies of man will involve a wide range of complicated facts, and a most comprehensive view of the circumstances of his nature and condition. Upon this probability alone, we should have suspected the accuracy of M. Canard's reasonings, who compresses the statement into very great simplicity indeed, and resolves the whole explanation into a sort of arithmetical estimate.

The increase of national wealth is occasioned by the permanent excess of the annual produce above the annual consumption; and this excess is determined by the prevalence of economy above extravagance; of the disposition to save and accumulate, above the passion for expense. When a nation is in this active, healthful, and flourishing condition, it gains from all other nations, according to M. Canard, an annual balance of trade proportioned to the surplus of its produce above its own consumption. This balance must ultimately be paid in the precious metals; and the increase of money, instead of being received into the channels of circulation by an augmentation of prices, is invested as an addition to productive capital or stock. In this, however, there is a natural and necessary limit. In proportion as the balance of trade increases, the competition of capitalists gradually lowers the rate of interest, as well as the profits of stock. But, in proportion as the rate of interest and profit is lowered, there is the less temptation to employ surplus wealth in the shape of capital; and, of course, there is the greater temptation to spend it as revenue. The augmentation of national wealth has a constant tendency, therefore, to discourage the spirit of accumulation, and to encourage the spirit of expense. The latter must ultimately become predominant over the former; the annual consumption will then exceed the annual produce; the balance of trade will be permanently unfavourable; and the nation will be impoverished and ruined, in a progression exactly the converse of that by which it had previously attained to wealth and grandeur. Thus, according to our author, the gradual diminution of profits and interest is at once the effect of increasing riches, and the proximate cause of that growing expenditure which swallows up all riches; and thus nations are represented as if fated to revolve for ever in a circle.

Before pointing out the fallacy of this piece of reasoning, we cannot refrain from expressing our surprise, that an author, who appears conversant with the most recent improvements of political science, should assume the reality of a balance of trade; more especially as the supposition does not form an indispensable part of his argument. That decrease in the interest of money and the rate of profits, which he views in so singular a light, might surely take place in a country which confined itself to its own inland trade, studiously avoiding the relations of foreign commerce. And there is no absurdity in believing that the balance of produce and consumption might lean either to one side or the other, in a kingdom bounded, as Berkeley has supposed, by a brazen wall of a thousand cubits. There is no need of a balance of foreign trade, paid in the precious metals, in order to realize that surplus of the annual produce, which, in a thriving country, is added to the mass of accumulated stock. The addition is made by an actual distribution of this surplus among the industrious classes of the people: for the only difference between what he now denominates accumulation, and what we strictly call consumption, is, that the consumers are different; being, in the one case, totally unproductive of value, and, in the other, replacing what they consume.

If, in the foregoing argument of M. Canard, it were true, that

67

the lowering of profits operates as a discouragement to the farther investiment of capital, it would not be a just inference, that a progressive decline of national wealth must ensue. We should only be warranted to infer this, that the increase of national wealth had a *maximum*; that there was a point, beyond which the amount of capital, productively employed, could receive no augmentation. Every accession of wealth to the nation, over and above that amount, would be spent and consumed as revenue; because there was no temptation of profit to employ it in the form of stock: But that amount of capital would still be maintained, because, up to that point, there was an adequate profit derived from it. There would be no diminution, therefore, of the national capital, and no progressive decline of wealth. The annual produce and annual consumption would be equally balanced; the condition of the people would be stationary.

But it is very far from being true, that the diminution of profits, which originates in an increased competition of capitals, operates as a discouragement to the farther investment of capital. It is in this particular that the author appears to have misled himself through the reasonings of the present chapter. Competition unquestionably regulates profits, as well as the other elements of price. But the only reason why an increased competition lowers the rate of profit, is, that, in consequence of an enlarged capital, the amount of profits, upon the whole, is increased. A greater quantity of stock draws a larger sum of profits; that is, the motive to invest capital increases with the increase of capital. An augmentation of the stock, which is productively invested, is followed by a fall in the rate of profit; only because the actual profits, as now extended, admit of being abridged, without destroying the motive to continue that investment. And this fall of the rate, instead of causing a diminution in the amount of profits, is itself only an effect of these profits having previously been increased, and is, in fact, no more than a return towards their former amount. After a reduction of the rate has taken place, it may be said that the motive to employ a certain specific sum is less than it was. But that forms no objection; because the reduction can only take place, when the circumstances of the country are such, that the stock of all the capitalists has, upon an average, received a proportionate augmentation. That augmentation arises out of an excess of the annual produce above consumption, which depends upon natural habits of industry and economy, and must, of course, diffuse an increase equably among the various individual capitals, of which the national capital is composed.

The present circumstances of the world, in general, or of any

68

particular nation, do not permit us to anticipate a period at which the enlargement of productive capital can be supposed to attain a *maximum*. Such is the re-action of expense and reproduction upon each other, that, in order to define that *maximum* in general terms, it would previously be necessary to assign the ultimate limit, both of produce and of consumption. But the prolific virtue of the soil, as well as the effective powers of industry, the numbers of the human species, as well as the multiplication of luxurious wants, have each of them a range of possible extension, which, to our apprehension, must be pronounced indefinite.

We cannot pretend to explain the contents of the *sixth* chapter. It is entitled, *General Point of View*, and is occupied with a long suffocating parallel, between the circulation of merchandize and money, in opposite currents or canals, and, what is held to be perfectly similar, the circulations of venous and arterial blood in the vascular system. It is a simile of about twenty pages, and is introduced to the indulgence of the reader, by the following expressions.

'On a vu ci-dessus l'espèce de similitude qu'il y a entre la circulation du sang et celle du travail. *Prolongeons* cet aperçu *autant qu'il peut s'étendre*, et analysons tous les traits de ressemblance qu'il y a entre ces deux espèces de circulation. Il est nécessaire auparavant d'exposer le tableau de la circulation du sang.' p. 107.

An offence of such magnitude, against all the rules both of taste and of scientific method, lies beyond the reach of our animadversion, being quite unprovided for in the criminal code of criticism. We shall therefore content ourselves with remarking, that scarcely any subject has been more unfortunately exposed to injudicious analogy, than that of the circulation of money. This very title, indeed, involves a false metaphor. In an article of our former Number,* we pointed out a singular mistake, into which Dr Smith has been led, by admitting certain figurative expressions into his reasonings, with regard to paper-money. Another proof occurs at present to our recollection, of the folly of indulging in these analogies, however briefly they may be stated. Dr Smith, in his Wealth of Nations, calls money 'the great *wheel* of circulation,' and paper-money 'a new and less expensive wheel.' Mr Hume says, in his Political Discourses, 'money is *none* of the wheels of trade; it is the *oil* which renders the motion of the wheels more smooth and easy.'

The *seventh* chapter treats of *States in their mutual relations*. It contains a tolerably distinct abridgment of those reasonings and

* *Vide* p. 179.

illustrations, by which Dr Smith has exposed the errors of the mercantile system. We mean to say, that it is immediately abridged from the Wealth of Nations; though M. Canard makes no acknowledgment of this. It was with much pleasure that we found those liberal and enlightened maxims, with respect to the foreign relations of commerce, in a work which has been sanctioned by the approbation of the National Institute. At the present important crisis, the prevalence of such views, among the leading statesmen of France, might prove of permanent and essential benefit to the world.

In the first part of the *eighth* chapter, the title of which is *Taxation*, he professes to resolve very clearly the question proposed by the Institute, to which he gives a decided negative. He endeavours to show, that taxes diffuse themselves equally over all the different branches of revenue, on whatever branch they may nominally be imposed; and whether they are levied at the source of revenue or upon consumption. But, of this proposition, he has not presented any proof which to us appears satisfactory. He explains his argument by stating a case. The rent of land, he assumes, is settled, like the price of any commodity, by the reciprocal competition of the landlord or seller, and of the farmer or buyer. If, at the moment when they are about to conclude a bargain, the state imposes a tax upon rent, their reciprocal competition will still operate in such a manner that this tax will be equally shared between the two. What is true of the landlord and farmer, is true of all persons in the relation of buyer and seller; and every tax, affecting the subject of sale, will be proportioned between them, whether it be nominally imposed on the one or upon the other. But if this holds with regard to a single buyer and a single seller, a little consideration will satisfy us, that it must hold equally with regard to a succession of many buyers and sellers; and whether the tax be imposed upon the original seller, or upon the first consumer, or upon any one of the intermediate purchasers, it will, in all cases, be proportionally paid by all. Now, this argument is certainly erroneous; inasmuch as it proceeds upon the assumption, that the contract between a proprietor of land and his farmer is exactly of the same kind with a bargain about any vendible commodity. The contrary of this is a point very clearly ascertained; and about which even those writers are agreed, who are most hostile to the project of a territorial impost; and who deny, most confidently, the ultimate incidence of taxes upon the neat produce of land. The rent which accrues to the landlord, is all that portion of the produce, however great or however small it may be, which remains after the whole stock or expenses of the farmer are

70

replaced, together with their profits at the usual rate. The whole effect of competition on the part of the landlord is, that he shall draw no less than this surplus; the whole effect of competition on the part of the farmer is, that the landlord shall draw no more. But what the amount of that surplus may be, depends neither upon the landlord nor the farmer, but upon the fertility of the earth and the bounty of nature. When a tax, therefore, is imposed, which directly affects the bargain between these two parties, it never can be shared between them; because the farmer already derives no more from the land than the replacement of his stock, with its necessary profits: any part of the tax that he might be supposed to pay would, in truth, form an additional advance, for which it would be necessary that he should be reimbursed. The whole tax is a certain annual expense, a certain portion of capital annually advanced, the whole of which must be replaced out of the annual reproduction, before the surplus or neat produce can be set aside for the landlord. Instead of being shared between him and the farmer, it is wholly deducted from that surplus which constitutes the rent.

We are rather inclined to believe, that the same train of reasoning, which thus proves that all taxes on land are paid by the proprietor alone, requires very little extension, in order to lead us to a more general conclusion, that all taxes whatever ultimately fall on the neat surplus of the annual reproduction. The argument, perhaps, has not yet been stated in such a form as to leave no room for objection; but this proposition appears to us the nearest approximation to truth, that has yet been offered upon the subject. It forms a necessary part, as most of our readers must be aware, of the system maintained by the followers of Quesnai; but, in the examination of that system by its antagonists, and even in the illustration of it by its most intelligent admirers, a line of distinction has not always been sufficiently marked between the theoretical conclusion, or general fact, of the ultimate incidence of taxes, and the practical scheme of a direct territorial tax. For ourselves, we will confess, that, while we entertain more than doubts with respect to the expediency of the latter, we have very little hesitation as to the truth of the former. At any rate the one is not a necessary inference from the other; for, in proceeding to discuss the practicability of that project, other principles and views of political economy must be brought into consideration. Though taxes are finally paid out of the neat produce, it may perhaps be more expedient that they should be drawn from it circuitously than directly: because the productiveness of a tax is not the only circumstance to which a wise statesman will attend; and because

71

it is not quite demonstrated, that a circuitous tax must be less productive than a direct one.

But although the territorial incidence of all taxes does not appear to suggest necessarily a direct impost upon land, which is the great practical tenet of the economists, it is intimately and necessarily connected with their great theoretical tenet, as to the source of national riches. These two positions, indeed, are involved in each other; or rather they may be said to form two views of the same general fact, one of which presents it indirectly. Reflecting upon this circumstance, of the logical relation that apparently subsists between these two assertions, it has sometimes struck us as a sort of presumptive evidence in favour of the economical theory, that each of them had separately presented itself to reflecting minds, long before the French philosophers had incorporated them together in a systematic demonstration. It may be said of all great and permanent discoveries, which have unfolded the operations of nature, that some occasional gleams of light broke out from time to time, before the full truth was revealed. The whole history of the mathematical and physical sciences forms a continued illustration of this remark. Nor does it fail to be true in those branches of knowledge which are supposed to present a less appropriate field of discovery. In the philosophy of mind, for example, the great fact of association was obscurely perceived by Hobbes, and even by Aristotle; the true theory of abstract signs was almost in possession of the schoolmen: Some of the French grammarians had nearly approached that interesting fact in the history of language which Mr Horne Tooke has the full merit of having ascertained: And, not to multiply instances too much, the two great discoveries by which Mr Hume and Bishop Berkeley have effected such a memorable revolution in metaphysics, the correct analysis of our ideas of cause, and the precise limitation of our knowledge of external substances, may be traced, the former in the writings of Barrow and Aquinas, the latter in the sceptical system of Democritus. The political economist might adduce similar instances from the history of his science. That doctrine of commercial freedom, the rapid progress of which sheds so much lustre on the enlightened practice of the present age, presented itself to the mind of Fenelon, secluded, at a vast distance from the vulgar details of business, in the retreats of literature and religion. By a still more remarkable coincidence, the same truth was distinctly apprehended and zealously maintained by Sir Dudley North,* who had passed his life in the prac-

* We allude to a very remarkable passage in the life of Lord Keeper Guildford, by Roger North, p. 167.

tical occupations of trade, at a time when the commercial system was loudly and successfully recommended to all the legislatures of Europe, both by merchants and by speculative economists. That principle, with regard to the primary and essential source of wealth, the elucidation of which has given political economy a new form, or rather first gave a strict scientific form to that subject, has been detected in some obscure authors, whose names and writings are now only sought after on account of this casual anticipation: It is likewise stated in a much more remarkable manner by a philosopher of antiquity, whose name once exercised a despotic authority, and whose writings have for some time sunk into unmerited neglect.* The curious fact also which suggested these reflections, that of the ultimate incidence of all taxes upon the neat produce of land, was very distinctly perceived by Mr Locke. It may be considered, we have already said, as a sort of presumption for the truth of the economical theory, that the two propositions of which it consists, and which are intimately connected with each other, had thus separately and independently occurred to the most cultivated understandings, by which, in former times, the relations of political economy were examined.

The most correct and regular demonstration, therefore, of the territorial incidence of taxes, would consist in a deduction of that evidence on which the fundamental principle of Quesnai's system exists. As the full development of this analysis, however, would occupy a larger space than is consistent with the plan of the present article, we shall present the subject in an indirect form, which, within the limits to which we are confined, may be better adapted to the majority of our readers. We intend to show, that, in the celebrated treatise of Dr Smith, though that author denies the ultimate incidence of taxes upon land, the principles which he has established involve this conclusion. That Smith did not precisely distinguish the real import of the economical system, is now confessed, we believe, even by those who agree with him in rejecting it. We are further satisfied that he derived a much larger portion of his reasonings from them, than he himself perhaps recollected; that his principles on the formation and distribution of national riches approached more nearly to those of Quesnai, than he was himself aware; and that, to have recognised an entire coincidence, it was only necessary for him to have followed out his analysis a few steps farther.

In that amusing, but not very instructive part of the Wealth of Nations, which treats of taxation, it is admitted, in the first place, that no tax can fall upon the wages of labour; though even

* *Vid.* Arist. de Repub. I. 8.–12.

73

advanced by the labourer, it must be replaced to him by his employer, and is therefore finally paid either out of the profits of stock, or out of the rent of land. It is farther admitted, that no tax can fall upon the profits of stock: Though advanced by the employer of stock, it must be replaced to him, either by the consumers in an augmented price, or by the landlord in a diminished rent, or by the monied capitalist in a diminished rate of interest. But the interest of money differs in no respect from the immediate profits of stock; it is precisely of the same nature; and, in the operations of national wealth, is governed by the same rules. All taxes, therefore, whether imposed upon the wages of labour, or upon the profits of stock, are finally paid, either by the consumers in an increase of price, or by the landlord in a diminution of rent. Now, the consumers compose the whole population of the state; they can only pay taxes, as they pay all the other parts of price, out of their respective revenues; and these revenues must be derived from wages, from profit, or from rent. But no taxes can ultimately fall, either on profit or on wages; wherefore those, which are levied on consumers, are all ultimately paid from rent. We are thus led, from the admissions of Dr Smith, to conclude, that all taxes, however levied, are finally incident upon the neat produce, and are ultimately paid by the landlord either in a diminution of his rent, or in an increase of the wages and prices which, out of his actual rent, he distributes among the other classes of the community.

The remainder of M. Canard's eighth chapter is occupied with a disquisition on the best form of taxation, and on the effects with which every new tax is accompanied upon the general system of circulation. The observations which compose this disquisition, though in our opinion fundamentally erroneous, will be useful in suggesting to the reader several points of view, from which the theory of finance may, with advantage, be considered. The author's conclusions, however, are all derived from that principle of the equal diffusion of taxes, on which we have already stated our opinion. It has conducted him to several results, which, though by no means new, are very different from the ideas in which the most judicious writers on finance appear at present to acquiesce: such as, that the most expedient taxes are those which are imposed upon the necessaries of the poor; that in whatever manner a tax be placed, its effects upon the various branches of industry, and employments of stock, will ultimately adjust themselves in a perfect equilibrium; that, until this equilibrium is restored, every tax must be attended with the various inconveniences that result from an artificial derangement in the system of competition and exchanges; and that, therefore, every old tax is good, and every new tax pernicious. Some of these positions appear inconsistent with each other; and all of them might be shown, from various considerations, to be full of error. But it is unnecessary, we hope, to enter into a more formal confutation of them, than that which is implied in the remarks we have already made on the principles from which they have been derived by our author.

The *last* chapter treats of the *Funding System*, and presents a mixture of judicious observations, with some very unsound maxims of policy. The practice of loans, or anticipations of the public revenue, is justified by the expediency of distributing unusual advances over a succession of years, both in order to equalize the annual expenditure, and to secure a prompt supply upon occasions of emergency. With reference to the practicability of the funding system, M. Canard considers nations under several different points of view,—as territorial, and as commercial states; and, under each of these two aspects, as in a stationary, advancing, or declining condition. For the remarks which he has brought together in this discussion, we must refer our readers to the original work, in which they will derive some instruction, and some amusement, from the geometrical precision with which he successively considers the several cases in this series of suppositions. The most prominent and the most objectionable of his positions is deduced from those reasonings, contained in the fifth chapter, of which we have already endeavoured to expose the fallacy. As nations, according to him, may acquire a surplus of wealth above what can possibly be employed as capital, and as it is this surplus which destroys the national spirit of accumulation, and undermines the national prosperity, the funding system, or the art of loans, presents itself as a most salutary expedient for absorbing the superfluity, and, by consequence, for retarding the commencement of national decline. Every loan, therefore, (for M. Canard cannot refuse a metaphor), is a wholesome bleeding, which relieves the political body from a plethoric malady. And he does not scruple to deliver it as his opinion, that if it had not been for those financial operations, by which England has accumulated her immeasureable debt, the superabundance of wealth would long ago have plunged her into that course of decline, from which, even in spite of her funding system, she cannot long be preserved. After the strictures which we formerly made on the principle from which these conclusions are derived, we deem it unnecessary to offer any further repetition of them. They appear a match to any of the speculative follies to which the national debt

75

has given birth. When we consider at once M. Canard's attachment to professional forms, and his unquestionable knowledge of the principles of political economy, we may reasonably be surprised that these consequences, on the subject of the funding system, did not strike him as a *reductio ad absurdum* of his theory, with regard to the necessary decline of national wealth.

Upon the whole, if we leave this work with a favourable impression, it is less from any permanent utility which we conceive it to possess, than from the specimen it affords of the talents of the author. He shows a more extensive acquaintance with economical speculations, than has always appeared in the books that have recently been brought to this country from France,—though we have found it necessary, on several occasions, to point out errors which more accurate reading would have enabled him to avoid. There is also a considerable degree of ingenuity in the turn which he has given to certain discussions; but we do not find that his peculiar mode of considering them has conducted him to any new results, or has enabled him to make any addition to our stock of political truths. Some advantage, however, is gained by a careful and even minute examination of such publications; because we are forced to recur to our first principles, and to undertake a scrutiny of the propositions in which we have formerly acquiesced. By frequent retrospects of this kind, we are placed in firmer possession of the discoveries that have been made; and the boundary of our real acquisitions is more accurately delineated. It has been the aim of the foregoing criticism to assist such of our readers as may be disposed to examine, in this strict manner, the memoir of M. Canard.

Vol. II ([No. IV] July 1803), Art. XI (pp. 402–421).
Thoughts on the Restriction of Payments in Specie at the Banks of England and Ireland. By Lord King. London, May 1803. pp. 106. 8vo.

THIS sensible and instructive publication contains the substance of what was urged in Parliament, by Lord King, against the last renewal of the Bank Restriction Bills. His reasoning coincides, at least in its general outline, with that of Mr Boyd's well known pamphlet: setting out with the strong presumptions which might have led us to expect an excessive issue of paper, and confirming that probability by a reference to the price of bullion, and the rate of foreign exchange. We must acknowledge, however, that the argument is presented by Lord King in a more corrected form, as well as with more candour. And the interval of experience that has now elapsed, has furnished him with a larger body of evidence, and a variety of additional illustrations.

Though from the very first, there could be no doubt of the impolicy and injustice of the restriction; yet, at the date of Mr Boyd's letter, the measure was too recent to warrant a confident opinion with regard to its particular influence on prices. It was, in its kind, quite novel and unexampled; and its operation was necessarily affected by many complicated circumstances. But now, it may be affirmed, that of all the political experiments which the temerity of statesmen ever hazarded, there is not another which has been more fairly tried than this, or of which the result has been ascertained with greater certainty. We have had an opportunity of observing the operation of the measure, under many varieties of situation, and where almost every circumstance has been successively varied, by which it might either have been counteracted or assisted; in war and in peace, in famine and in plenty, with a favourable and with an unfavourable balance of trade, during a languid stagnation of our manufactures, and amidst the spirit and heat of speculation. Throughout all these changes, one uniform effect may be perceived; which, with the evidence by which it is proved, and the reasonings by which it is explained, is very ably and perspicuously described by Lord King. For the information of our readers, on this most interesting subject, we shall make an abstract of his publication; because it is highly important that the public should at length entertain a correct opinion, with respect to those laws which have vitiated the currency of this country. We shall endeavour to convey the substance of his reasonings, without meaning to confine ourselves to his language, or to the precise order in which he has arranged the different steps of the argument.

It does not appear to have ever been doubted by any of the writers on political economy,* that an enlargement of paper currency, beyond the growing demands of trade, has exactly the same operation in raising prices, as a multiplication of the precious metals. There is this difference, indeed, between the two cases, that the one is a local effect merely, whereas the other extends over the whole commercial world; and that the latter is produced gradually, scarcely becoming sensible till after the lapse of a considerable period of time; whereas the former may take place very quickly, and has actually been known to take place very quickly in more instances than one. It is evident, that every such rise in the money price of commodities, is, in other words, a fall in the commodity price, or exchangeable value of money. It is likewise established by experience, and before actual experience might have been inferred from the nature of the thing, that every such depreciation of the value of the circulating medium, is accompanied with much inconvenience and distress. These are the more severe, the shorter the period of time is within which the depreciation has been effected. The value of monied capital is diminished, and the livelihood is injured, of all those persons whose income is limited to a fixed sum of money. If a considerable depreciation takes place within a short period of time, the grossest injustice likewise must unavoidably ensue, with regard to the performance of all contracts previously agreed on. It is on all these accounts of high political importance, that the circulating medium of every country should preserve a steady and uniform value; and this it can never do, unless the effective currency, which is a quantity compounded of the actual amount, and of the rate of circulation,† preserves permanently the same proportion to the demands of commerce.

Every banking company or private banker, by whom paper is issued, lies under great temptations of issuing it to excess; in the same manner as other traders are liable to overstrain their credit, or to overstock the market. Besides the direct profit which a bank derives from the circulation of its notes, they afford facilities, which the most cautious banker cannot always refuse, either to his own speculations, or to those of his confidential correspondents. In point of fact, nothing can be more certain, than that these temptations often get the better of all their prudence. But while our currency remained in its natural and sound condition, the excess of paper circulation could never be carried so far as to have

* See our First Volume, p. 179.
† See our First Volume, p. 178.

78

any general and public effect upon prices. By means of the instant convertibility into specie, the superfluous paper was very speedily returned back upon the issuer, as soon as it began to undergo the smallest degree of depreciation. But the condition of our currency, can no longer be considered as sound or natural, when the convertibility into specie is dispensed with; and, after this check is removed, there is no longer any limit of the excess to which paper, while it retains the confidence of the country, may be carried. Mr Thornton, in his excellent work, has explained in what manner the higher branches of national currency regulate and limit the rest; gold and silver, all paper circulation; and the paper of the Bank of England that of all the country banks.* If to the present suspension of cash payments at the Bank of England, another law were added, relieving the country banks from the obligation of converting their notes into those of the Bank of England, there would no longer exist any check to the emission of country paper; and there would be no bounds to the excess in which every banker might indulge, so long as his credit and solvency were unimpaired. Even in such an extreme case, however, the country paper would not possess a more extensive licence than that which the paper of the Bank of England enjoys at present; and the effectual salutary limitation to which the country paper is at present subjected, is founded exactly upon the same principle with that which formerly controuled the Bank of England, under the obligation of converting its notes into specie. From the moment that the unwise law of 1797 discharged the Bank from this most necessary obligation, nothing remained to controul its discretion, or to impose any boundary to the extent of its paper circulation. The directors of this company are at all times susceptible of the same temptations to which other traders are exposed; they have been known sometimes to yield to these, even under the checks and controuls of the ancient system; and now that all these are removed, it would be in the highest degree credulous and absurd to expect that they will decline the opportunity of increasing the profits of their stock. These profits, it is well known, arise principally from the circulation of their notes.

It is from the operation of gold and silver, in confining paper within its proper bounds, that the constant and immediate convertibility of notes into specie is rendered an indispensable condition, in every sound system of currency. This is a principle in the theory of money, which has hitherto been very imperfectly understood, even by those who, in other respects, have explained it most fully. To the deficiency of all our systematic writers upon this

* See our First Volume, p. 190.

point, we are inclined to ascribe the opposite extremes of error, which with equal confidence, and equal loudness, are maintained, respecting the present state of our circulating medium. In the provinces, among our landed proprietors, and from that description of our parliamentary representatives, we still, as of old, hear most ignorant declamations against country banks, and all paper currency. In the great commercial cities, and especially in the metropolis, opinions are gravely avowed, by persons who ought to be acquainted at least with the details of the money trade, that the precious metals are altogether unnecessary, even as a part of circulation; and that the provisional law of 1797 should be established as a permanent system. If the former sentiment may be classed among the expiring prejudices of the vulgar, this visionary scheme betrays no less ignorance of political œconomy, and in its practical tendency is much more pernicious. It is not, however, to be treated as a doctrine entirely new, or as for the first time suggested by the existing circumstances of this country. If authority could yield any support to so palpable an error, the sanction might be found of other names, than it will probably be able to produce in the present day. An idea of this sort runs through the Querist of Bishop Berkeley, not the least remarkable production of that acute genius; from whose fame it cannot be considered a derogation, that, among many original and valuable views upon a science then almost uncultivated, some errors are to be found, from which we are not completely guarded by all the discoveries and experience of subsequent times. He appears to have conceived*, that all circulation is alike a circulation of credit, whether metal or paper be employed as the medium; and that as coined metals were, in the progress of mankind from barbarism, substituted for barter, so, in a farther stage of improvement, a paper medium is to be substituted for coin. If the question were solely, Whether it may be stated in the abstract as at all practicable, to carry on the business of internal commerce by a medium of circulation merely conventional, neither possessing intrinsic value itself, nor immediately convertible into a commodity of intrinsic value? we should answer this question in the affirmative. The practicability is sufficiently proved, by the experiment which has been made in this country; and there existed no reason, *à priori*, to doubt its possibility. But the real and important question is a very different one: How far this practicable scheme is, by motives of expediency, and after a full view of its operation, recommended to be actually carried into practice? To this we

* See Numbers 426, 439, 441, and 445, of the Querist, a work originally published in 1735.

have no less hesitation in pronouncing a negative, upon the principle which has already been explained. A perfect system of currency must be composed both of specie and paper.

The introduction of paper money, the most refined, perhaps, of all the expedients to which the relations of society have given birth, was not only an immense step in the progress of commerce, but may be considered as having marked an epoch in the history of mankind. But the essential benefit of the invention does not consist, as Berkeley supposed, in forming an entire substitution for metallic currency; but, in saving a certain portion of so costly an article, and, what is of far greater consequence, in facilitating exchanges between places remote from each other, and economizing the time and the labour of large payments. Specie, however, as possessing intrinsic value, must still be considered as the ultimate element into which the currency of the country may at all times be resolved; and is the true basis upon which the fabric of paper circulation must be solidly reared. If the whole currency is merely conventional, no check operates against an excessive issue, and consequently no security exists for the permanent value of the medium of exchange. That permanency can only be secured, by making the conventional representative of value constantly and readily convertible into real value; constantly and readily convertible into gold and silver; because these preserve more steadily than other commodities, an uniform value. Upon the principle, which we have endeavoured to explain, the excess of paper circulation would be converted into whatever commodity the paper was made convertible, provided that commodity was of intrinsic value. But it cannot be rendered convertible into some commodities with the same convenience, as into others; nor would the restraint upon excessive issue operate, in every case, with the same degree of efficacy and regularity. As the precious metals form the most convenient measure of value and medium of exchange, when the whole circulation is effected by a medium of intrinsic value; for the same reasons, they are better fitted than any other commodity to be the basis of a conventional currency, and to form that real value into which every portion of it may at all times be immediately converted. Permanency of value, from age to age, is the point of first importance in the medium of circulation. And while the currency of a nation consists, either wholly of the precious metals, or of a paper system founded on, and secured by the principle of convertibility, its value cannot be considerably depreciated except, along with the currency of the whole commercial world, by the discovery of new mines of extreme fertility; an event so rare, as to have occurred only once within the period of historical memory, and that at the epoch when the two hemispheres of the earth were first revealed to each other.

The preceding observations are sufficient, we trust, to shew, that when a national Bank, whose notes form the chief branch of currency, is relieved from the obligation of payments in cash, the only controul is then removed which limits the issue of paper to what is actually required by trade. That with such an opportunity, and such a licence, no Bank will ever long resist the temptation of high profits and extraordinary gains, there are very obvious reasons to presume; yet it is a matter of some nicety to make out, in a particular instance, a distinct proof of the fact of undue issue. It is a case of that sort which scarcely admits of direct evidence. Even when we can obtain faithful documents of the amount of notes in circulation during a series of successive periods, we are not fully entitled to consider a progressive increase of amount as conclusive, unless that increase be very great indeed: because the quantity of currency required by the trade of a country varies with the rate of circulation; that rate of circulation differs with the different kinds of currency, and in each kind is liable to be accelerated or retarded by the various fluctuations of demand and of credit. Nor does a high and growing state of prices afford any more satisfactory proof of an undue excess in the quantity of circulating medium; because the state of prices is a very complex subject, and is known to us very vaguely; and because the same increase, which an excess of currency would occasion, may be produced by many other causes, such as a failure of produce or supply, or an accumulation of taxes, the operation of all which is so complicated together, that it is difficult to assign to any one its proper portion of the whole joint effect. Fortunately, however, there are two very simple and satisfactory tests, by which the fact of an excessive currency may be ascertained. The nature of these we took an opportunity of explaining in a former article of this Review*, at a time when we did not yet think that sufficient evidence was laid before the public to apply the inference, with conclusive certainty, to the conduct of the Bank of England.

When the circulating medium of a country has suffered a depreciation, whether it proceeds from the debasement of a metallic currency, or from the discredit, or from the excess, of a paper currency, the currency price of gold and silver bullion must rise, at the same time, with that of all other commodities. This fact is usually expressed by saying, that the market price of bullion exceeds its mint price. When the market price of bullion comes to

* Vol. I, p. 184, and p. 200.

82

exceed its mint price, in consequence of a depreciation of currency, the rate of foreign exchange will suffer a nominal and apparent fall. The domestic currency has sunk in its bullion value, while foreign currencies remain unaltered; the proportion, therefore, of the bullion value of the former, to that of the latter, is changed. But though this proportion is changed, the ancient numbers, expressing it, are still adhered to by merchants. There will thus be a great difference between the computed rate of exchange, and its real rate; and whether the actual difference be in favour of, or against, the country whose currency is depreciated, the apparent rate will always be computed so much more against it, or so much less in its favour, in proportion to the degree of that depreciation. The use of these two tests, in ascertaining the fact of a depreciated currency, may be explained by several remarkable instances. Before the reformation of the silver coin in King William's time, we are informed by Dr Smith, the exchange between England and Holland, computed according to the standard of their respective mints, was 25 *per cent.* against England; but the value of the current coin of England was, at that time, rather more than 25 *per cent.* below its standard value*. Before the reformation of our gold coin in 1772, the market price of bullion exceeded the mint price, and the rate of foreign exchange was depressed; even the exchange with France was 2 or 3 *per cent.* against England. It is understood that, at that time, the French coin, though worn, was not so degraded as the English, and was, perhaps, 2 or 3 *per cent.* nearer its standard. Very soon after the recoinage in 1772, the market price of bullion fell to the mint price, and there was a corresponding improvement in the course of exchange; the difference turned immediately in favour of England, and against France†. The issue of assignats, during the Revolution, depreciated the currency of France in a greater degree than was ever known in any other instance. In the course of little more than two years, accordingly, the exchange between London and Paris fell between 60 and 70 *per cent.* to the disadvantage of the latter place: and would probably have fallen still more, by the operation of new issues of assignats, if the war had not interrupted the commercial intercourse of the two countries.‡

It is not, indeed, from every rise in the market-price of bullion above its mint price, or from every fall in the course of foreign exchange, that we are entitled to infer a depreciation of currency. A temporary excess of the market-price of bullion above its mint

* Wealth of Nations. II. 215.
† Id. I. 62. and II. 215.
‡ Lord King, p. 37.

price may be produced, without any peculiarity in the state of currency, by a failure in the supply of bullion from the mines, by a great demand for it either at home or from abroad, and, above all, by what is called an unfavourable balance of trade. The high market-price, which these circumstances occasionally for a short time produce, may be farther augmented and prolonged, if the expences of foreign warfare, and the remittance of foreign subsidies, are aggravated by a failure of the most necessary produce. It was from this view of the subject, that, when we examined the valuable publication of Mr Thornton, we deemed it proper to suspend our opinion, with respect to the operation of Bank of England paper upon prices, until the various causes of foreign expenditure might be considered as having completed their full effect; while, at the same time, we declared that the question would be solved to our conviction, if the excess of the market-price of bullion should continue, after the balance of trade was restored in favour of this country. In the same manner, it is somewhat difficult to discriminate, whether an unfavourable course of exchange is real or only apparent. When it is only a few degrees below par, and has been observed only for a short period of time, it is scarcely possible to determine whether it is a real difference from an unfavourable balance of trade, or an apparent difference from a depreciation of our currency. But the longer the period of time is, during which even a small difference continues, the greater does the presumption always become, that it is only an apparent difference; and this presumption would be remarkably strengthened, if the difference were against a country which formerly enjoyed a favourable balance of trade, of which the manufactures and foreign commerce had suffered no diminution, but had advanced in prosperity, and which had recently adopted a change in the system of its currency, that might possibly lead to depreciation. It must farther be observed, that, how short soever the period may be during which the course of exchange is observed, if the difference from par is very great, and exceeds a certain limit, there is then every reason to believe that a certain portion at least of this difference is only apparent, and must be ascribed to a depreciation of currency. No person can imagine, for a moment, that, when the exchange against Paris was almost 70 *per cent.* under par, that the whole of this immense difference, or that more than a very small portion of it, was real, and arising from the balance of trade. Nor does any one believe that the present exchange of 16 *per cent.* against Dublin, which is nearly twice as great as the usual difference, does not in part originate in a recent depreciation of the currency of Ireland. There is, indeed, a natural and necessary limit to the real difference of exchange, as occasioned by the balance of trade. This difference never can exceed, as Lord King has observed,* 'what will be sufficient to pay the expences and profit of the merchant who exports precious metals to restore the balance.' The same thing was long ago pointed out by Sir William Petty; who informs us, that, about the year 1672, 15 *per cent*. was given for the remittance of money from Ireland into England: and the remark which he subjoins, admits of an exact application to present circumstances:—'Although, in truth, exchange can never be naturally more than the land and water carriage of money between the two kingdoms, and the insurance of the same upon the way, *if the money be alike in both places*.'† Lord King farther states, that this expence will probably seldom exceed 8 *per cent*. from London to the continent of Europe; which may therefore be considered as the utmost limit of an unfavourable exchange, in a regular state of things.

From the foregoing observations, which we have insensibly protracted to an unexpected length, it may be concluded, in general, (and this general conclusion we may be prepared to apply to such particular instances as shall present themselves,) that, where a steady excess of the market price of bullion above its mint price, and a great depression of the course of exchange, are permanent amidst the variation of all those circumstances which influence the balance of trade, the two effects must be referred to one common cause, a depreciation of currency. Without any farther proof, the inference is just and satisfactory. But if it be farther fortified by direct evidence and official documents, either of a fraudulent debasement of coin, or of an unwonted augmentation in the issue of paper, the conclusion becomes irresistable to every understanding, that does not set all evidence and demonstration at defiance.

The amount of Bank of England paper in circulation, prior to the suspension of cash payments, was, upon an average of three years ending in December 1795, 11,975,573*l*. For a considerable time after that measure had been resorted to, the Directors appear to have acted with caution and forbearance, as if not yet sure of their ground, and doubtful of the success of the experiment on which they were about to venture. To supply the place of the guineas that were thrown out of circulation, an additional quantity of small notes was no doubt necessary: which Mr Thornton has probably estimated too highly when he states the amount at two millions; because it was not found immediately necessary to issue so large an amount. Until the year 1799, however, the issue

* P. 31.
† Political Survey of Ireland, p. 71.

of bank notes did not much exceed thirteen millions. But about the middle of that year, as we find from the accounts laid before Parliament, the notes in circulation amounted to 13,759,940*l.*; and, before the end of the year, exceeded fourteen millions. In the course of the succeeding year, they were increased about a million and a half more. Our readers will recollect, that Mr Thornton endeavours to shew that the issues of the bank did not exceed the average sum to which they amounted before the law of restriction. He admits, that in December 1800 they were proved to amount to 15,450,970*l.*; but then he observes, that the Governor of the Company stated, in the following spring, to the House of Commons, that they had drawn in about a million and a half of that sum; so that, when the two millions of small notes were also deducted, there remained a sum almost exactly equal to the average of issues before the restriction. When we examine, however, the accounts which have from time to time been laid before Parliament, we find, so far from this being a correct statement of the fact, that in spring 1801, the issue of notes amounted to 16,365,206*l.*; which was still farther increased in the summer of 1802, to 16,747,300*l.* According to the last account presented to the House of Commons, the Bank of England notes in circulation amounted to 16,108,560*l.* If we compare this sum with the above average of three years, ending in December 1795, even after we add to the latter the whole two millions of which Mr Thornton speaks, and which seems a very large allowance, the present issue from the Bank will be found to exceed that which formerly was convertible into specie, by something less than one-sixth of the whole. If we consider the quick circulation which paper admits of, and the increase which an accelerated rate of circulation gives to the effective powers of currency, this addition of almost one-sixth, must be regarded as an immense augmentation of the mass of efficient currency.

While the issue of Bank of England notes was moderate and restrained, the market-price of bullion (particularly of silver bullion, which is a more certain standard than gold, because a more regular article of commerce) continued very nearly the same as its established price in our mint; sometimes rising a little above that, and sometimes falling a little below it, but speedily returning towards it from each deviation. In the summer of 1799, however, about the same time with the great increase of bank paper, a rapid and extraordinary advance took place in the market-price of bullion. That of silver rose at once to 5s. 8d., almost 10 *per cent.* above the mint price. It continued to rise along with the progressive increase of notes; and in 1801, when they exceeded sixteen millions, it was as high as 6s., more than 16 *per cent.*, and even as 6s. 1d. more than 17 *per cent.* above the mint price.

While the issue of Bank of England notes was moderate and restrained, the rate of exchange with Hamburgh continued in favour of this country, being from 3 to 5 *per cent.* above par. But in the summer of 1799, about the same time with the great increase of Bank paper, a very rapid fall took place. It fell at once to 32, about 8 *per cent.* below par; and continued to fall almost regularly, though not quite so regularly as the price of bullion rose, along with the progressive increase of notes. At the commencement of 1801, when they exceeded sixteen millions, the exchange with Hamburgh was as low as 29*l.* 10s., almost 16 *per cent.* below par.

These facts are highly curious and important; important to our own country in the present juncture, on account of the conclusion which they enforce respecting a most important object of national policy; important to the economist of every country and age, from the new light which they throw on one of the most difficult subjects in his science. The detail of these facts may be accurately considered, in a set of excellent tables which Lord King has subjoined to his work; and which, from their construction in parallel columns, exhibit, more distinctly than we have been able to describe, the remarkable correspondence between the variations in the quantity of Bank notes, and the variations in the price of bullion and rate of exchange. During the late suspension of hostilities, the exchange was somewhat improved, though it still continued apparently unfavourable to England; and the market price of bullion fell in some degree, though it still remained considerably above the mint price. These effects must be ascribed to the beneficial influence, even of a momentary pacification, upon the commercial relations of this country; and from all former experience, it may with confidence be inferred, that, had there not been an actual depreciation of our currency, the market price of bullion would have been on a level with its mint price; and the computed exchange, instead of being against us, would have appeared, as doubtless the real balance was, greatly in our favour. It is very ingeniously observed by Lord King, with reference to the state of things at the date of his publication—

'We have, at the present time, a striking instance of an exchange with the Continent at par, and in an improving state; while the price of bullion is between 9 and 10 *per cent.* higher than the mint price. This extraordinary difference is rendered intelligible by supposing Bank notes to be depreciated, and the real balance of trade very different from the nominal, but by no other hypothesis.' p. 35.

We have already alluded to the remarkable state of the exchange between Dublin and London. While that with the Continent has been so uniformly unfavourable, as we have described it, the exchange with Dublin has been all along increasing in favour of this country. But this exception in point of fact, forms an additional illustration and proof of the general principle. In the former regular state of things, while the obligation of converting paper into specie subsisted, the ordinary difference of exchange between London and Dublin was 8 *per cent.* against the latter. But this has undergone a material alteration, since the Bank of Ireland, as well as that of England, received a licence of issuing paper free from that obligation. If the Bank of Ireland had been more moderate in its abuse of this licence than the Bank of England, it is obvious that the currency of the former would have suffered a less depreciation than that of the latter, and there would consequently have been an apparent diminution in the difference of exchange. On the other hand, if the Bank of Ireland has been more extravagant in its abuse of that licence than the Bank of England, the currency of the former must have suffered a still greater depreciation than that of the latter, and there will consequently have been an apparent increase in the difference of exchange. Now, the actual case is, that there has been a very great increase in the difference of exchange; and, agreeably to that correspondence which the preceding reasonings entitle us to expect, the issue of notes from the Bank of Ireland has been greatly more enlarged than that of the Bank of England. For the detection of this fact, and of most reprehensible conduct on the part of the Directors of the Bank of Ireland, the public is indebted to the intelligence and activity of Lord King; upon whose motion, in the month of February last, the following document, which we insert entire, was laid before Parliament.

'Account of the Amount of Bank of Ireland Notes in circulation at different periods, (including Bills under 5*l.*) presented to the House of Lords, pursuant to an order dated February 1803.

1797.			£.	1802.			£.
January 1.	.	.	621,917	June 1. .	.	.	2,678,980
April 1. .	.	.	737,268	August 1.	.	.	2,628,958
June 1. .	.	.	808,612	October 1.	.	.	2,528,951
September 1. .		.	959,999	December 1. .		.	2,530,867
1801.				1803.			
April 1. .	.	.	2,266,471	February 1. .		.	2,633,864
May 1. .	.	.	2,405,214				
June 1. .	.	.	2,350,012				(p. 106.)

In the space of six years, it is thus proved, the paper currency of the Bank of Ireland has been augmented from 621,917*l.* to 2,633,864*l.*; and its notes at present in circulation exceed, more than four times, the amount of what were in circulation when the act of restriction was passed. During the same period the price of silver in Dublin has experienced a great advance, having varied from 6s. 6d. to 7s. Irish currency; an increase which, estimating the mint price at 5s. 7d., is from 14 to 20 *per cent*. The rate of exchange between Dublin and London has been also remarkably affected; the difference having progressively increased from $8\frac{2}{3}$, the ordinary difference, to 10, 12, 14, and even 16, to which it has risen since the publication of the present work. This proof, of the depreciation of the Bank of Ireland notes, has not been confined to the course of exchange with London; but is felt in the transactions of Dublin with many of the provincial towns, where those notes have not acquired a general circulation, the currency still consisting either of specie or of country notes. In consequence of this, and of the depreciated condition of the Dublin currency, there is an actual difference of exchange between Dublin and those towns. In Belfast, for instance, this is the case; and when a payment is there made in Bank of Ireland notes, an additional sum is paid proportional to the discount. To these statements of Lord King, we may add a fact exactly of the same nature, which has recently come to our knowledge; that when there is a money-transaction betwixt this country and those parts of the north of Ireland, where the notes of the National Bank are not in general circulation, the difference of exchange, instead of being computed at 15 or 16 *per cent*. as against Dublin, does not exceed 8 *per cent*., which was the ordinary exchange with Dublin, before the measure of restriction was resorted to. 'It is impossible, (our author observes), under such circumstances, to acquit the Directors of the Bank of Ireland of the charge of gross misconduct, even upon the ground of supposed ignorance and inexperience. An important trust, which, upon mistaken principles of political necessity, was committed to this corporate body by Parliament, for the public benefit, appears to have been perverted to the private interest of the proprietors of their stock.'—p. 53. The remedy which Lord King has proposed, for the cure of these disorders, appears extremely simple, and founded on the justest principles of political economy. While the Bank of England continues to enjoy the restriction, that of Ireland cannot, with any propriety or justice, be directed to resume the ancient system of payments in specie. But, as a temporary expedient, an obligation upon the Bank of Ireland to pay upon demand, in notes of the Bank of

England, would unquestionably impose upon the Irish Directors the necessity of restraining the issue of their paper, and of reducing it at least to the standard of English currency.

From the preceding mass of evidence, so harmoniously consistent with all the deductions of general principle, our readers, we trust, are prepared with us to pronounce, that the fact of a depreciation of our currency originating in excess, is completely established. To our mind, at least, the reasonings and statements of Lord King appear now quite decisive. We mean, decisive as to the actual consequences of the measure of 1797, and its pernicious influence upon the system of circulation. For of the impolicy of that measure, we never for a moment entertained a doubt. To have apprised the public of that, it was quite sufficient, that the most intelligent and best informed persons owned themselves unable at the time to descry its probable effects; and that it was in itself a violent interference of the Legislature, forcing the arrangements of commerce out of their accustomed and natural course. Nothing can be more judicious than the concluding observations of Lord King:

'A due regard to *general rules*, and especially to the great rules of property, forms a most important part of the duty of a legislator. They are the foundations of all private and political security; and the only means by which great principles can be effectually protected against rash speculation and hasty and inconsiderate judgments. A strict adherence to these rules, and a deep sense of their value and importance, is the great characteristic which distinguishes civilized nations, and which marks the progress of political knowledge and improvement. It has, in general, distinguished the legislative proceedings of our own country, and may be justly regarded as one of the principal causes of our national prosperity and greatness. Yet a more extraordinary deviation from all general rules has never occurred, than in that change in the system of our paper currency, which commenced in the Act of Suspension of 1797, and is still continued. A law to suspend the performance of contracts has been suffered to remain in force upwards of six years. A power has been committed to the Directors of the Bank, which is not entrusted by the constitution even to the Executive Government; a power of regulating, in a certain degree, the standard of the currency of the kingdom, and of varying this standard at their pleasure. A precedent has been established, by which, upon any suggestion of temporary expediency, the whole personal property and monied interests of the country may be committed to the discretion of a commercial Body not responsible to the Legislature, and not known to the Constitution.

'This extraordinary measure, which originated in embarrassment and temporary difficulties, has been suffered to continue from mere inadvertence. Neither the Public nor the Legislature appear to have considered to what consequences such proceedings ultimately tend. Had Parliament been called upon to authorise any of those direct frauds upon the currency which have often disgraced arbitrary governments; had it been recommended to them to raise the denomination, or to diminish the value of the current coin, there can be no doubt that such a proposal would have been rejected with indignation. Yet an abuse of the same nature has been established by law in this country. The power of reducing the value of the currency, by a silent and gradual depreciation, is more dangerous, from the very circumstance of its being less direct, and less exposed to observation.

'The true interests of government and the people are not really at variance. No advantage can possibly be obtained by the former, under any emergency, from any change in the system of currency, by which the public is injured. After the first momentary relief, government, so far from deriving any benefit from such violations of established rules, is obliged, like other consumers, to increase its expences, to multiply its loans and taxes, and to adapt its revenue to the enhanced price of labour and commodities. But this is only a small part of the evils that have uniformly been experienced by those nations which have had frequent recourse to such expedients. The abuse increases in strength, and a return to the former system is rendered more difficult by delay; public credit suffers; the revenue and resources fail; and what was at first a mere temporary accommodation, becomes finally a permanent cause of national weakness and decay. The case which is here supposed is extreme; but every instance of a discretionary power, by which the currency may be depreciated, has this tendency, and may ultimately produce these effects.' pp. 83–86.

We have purposely abstained from interrupting the deduction of the principal argument, by an allusion to any collateral views or incidental topics, in which we feel ourselves disposed to differ from the author, or to criticise his mode of statement. It is proper that we should now explain very briefly the few objections which have occurred to us.

He has not, perhaps, adhered with exact precision to the distinction, of which, in the abstract, he seems aware, between the two sorts of depreciation; the one originating from excess, the other from discredit: For he appears to apprehend, that the excess alone of Bank of England notes might at length produce a discount between them and gold coin; (p. 37. & p. 81.) This seems inaccurate. It must be recollected, that paper cannot become permanently excessive, until gold and silver coin have been in a great measure thrown out of the channel of circulation. Every superfluous issue is, for some time, counteracted, in its influence on prices, by a displacement and exportation of an equivalent portion of precious coin: And when these are at length so much thrown out of circulation, that the fresh emissions of paper produce an uncorrected influence upon prices, the currency must then be considered, with regard to every sensible effect, as consisting entirely of paper. What remains of precious coin, forms, comparatively, no part of the circulating medium. Now, it is only between two different kinds of currency, bearing a sensible proportion to each other, that a discount can be established; a discount between the two different currencies of one place, being exactly the same thing as the course of exchange between the currencies of two different places. When a discount is established between the two currencies of one and the same place, it must proceed from a discredit or want of confidence in one of them; in consequence of which, two money-prices are recognized for all commodities, and the precious coins remain still in the channel of circulation, notwithstanding continued emissions of paper. We have little doubt that the discount at Dublin originated in this manner.

In the course of this author's liberal remarks on country banks, he gives an opinion in favour of that law which formerly prohibited the issue of notes under the value of five pounds. We are rather inclined to doubt the policy on which this prohibition was founded. The authority of Dr Smith indeed is with Lord King; but the principle of commercial freedom has such firm hold of our conviction, that, to warrant any exception from it, we should require much stronger reasons than are furnished upon this point by either of these writers.

Lord King has stated, rather too absolutely, perhaps, (p. 15. and p. 23.), that the circulating medium of a nation bears no proportion to its wealth and trade. It is quite true, that the number of exchanges bears no *ratio* to the mere quantity or amount of circulating medium; because the quantity required varies, as we have often observed, with the rate or velocity of circulation. But the amount of circulating medium, and the rate of circulation, may be taken together, and considered as forming a complex quantity; and then there can be no doubt that this complex quantity bears a *ratio* to the number and value of exchanges. This *ratio*, it is evident, may be fixed and constant, though the two component parts of that complex quantity are perpetually varying; because, while trade continues the same, they must vary inversely as each other. Nor does it affect the truth of this proposition, as thus stated abstractedly, that the present resources of political arithmetic do not yet enable us to assign the *ratio*.

Lord King has endeavoured to strengthen that part of his argument, which is founded on the unfavourable state of foreign exchange, by a theory which, as far as we know, is quite new; that,

in the present commercial relations of Great Britain, the real
course of exchange with the Continent must necessarily and permanently be in our favour. The great trade with the East Indies
and China is carried on almost entirely by an exportation of silver
to Asia, and this trade is possessed almost exclusively by Great
Britain. We must therefore draw from the rest of the western
world, that supply of this precious metal which is annually con-
signed to the east. Our direct commerce with Spain and Portugal
is inadequate to this purpose: we must derive the supply, therefore, from the several nations of the Continent, among whom the
annual produce of the mines is distributed from Portugal and
Spain. This bullion we can only purchase by an exportation either
of produce or of manufactured goods; our exports of these, to
those nations, must therefore constantly exceed our import of
goods and produce from the same nations. The balance of trade
with the Continent is thus, it is said, necessarily and permanently
in our favour; and of course, likewise, the difference of exchange.
The plausibility of this theory at first caught our assent; but, on
farther consideration, we were led to suspect that it involves a
fallacy. It does not follow, because our imports always consist
partly of bullion, that the balance of trade is therefore permanently
in our favour. Bullion is a commodity for which, like every other,
there is a varying demand; and which, exactly like any other, may
enter the catalogue either of imports or exports; and this exportation or importation of bullion will not affect the course of
exchange in a different way from the exportation or importation
of other commodities. The real course of exchange, between two
countries, depends upon the state of their reciprocal credits and
debits. When the real difference is in favour of this country, it
must be occasioned by the demand abroad for bills being greater
than the supply; and that difference is no other than the premium
which is paid for bills, in consequence of the competition. This
excess in the demand abroad above the supply of such bills,
proceeds from an excess of the debts due to us, above the debts due
by us; that is, from an excess of our whole exports above our
whole imports. The balance thus due to us, and which cannot be
liquidated by means of bills, may either be discharged by sending
bullion to this country, or may be allowed to remain for a time
unpaid. So long as it remains a permanent debt, the price of bills
will continue high, that is, the course of exchange will continue in
our favour. If the balance be discharged by an actual transference
of bullion, the supply of bills abroad will then become equal to the
demand, and exchange will be at par. But even when it has the
effect of liquidating such a balance, bullion is only sent to this

country, because there is an effectual demand for it, which allows the importation; and it liquidates that balance in no other way than an equal import of any other commodity, for which there had been a demand, would have done. The state of exchange, therefore, does not depend upon the bullion trade, more than upon that of any other commodity; it depends entirely on the balance of debts. Provided the whole exports are no more than equal, during a given period of time, to the whole imports, the exchange will be at par, although a great part, the greater part, or even the whole of those imports, may have consisted of bullion. Let it be supposed, for example, that the commerce between Britain and Portugal had consisted wholly of woollen cloths exported from Britain, and of nothing but bullion directly imported from Portugal, provided the whole quantity of woollen cloth exported was no more than equal in value annually, to the whole quantity of bullion imported, and that the reciprocal purchases were made upon the same terms, in respect of the length of credit, the real exchange would have remained steadily at par, though we imported nothing but bullion; and if, on the other hand, our import of bullion had exceeded our export of woollen cloth; or if the Portuguese merchant had granted a more indulgent credit than he received from Britain, the course of exchange would then have been permanently against this country, although we imported nothing but bullion. That there is a steady influx of bullion into this country, both for our own consumption, and for the supply of our Asiatic trade; and that the course of exchange, until the year 1799, was steadily in favour of this country with almost the whole of the Continent; are facts which appear to us quite unconnected with each other. That favourable difference of exchange ought, perhaps, to be considered as having been partly apparent and partly real. That portion of it which was only apparent, was owing to the excellent state of our currency (for the gold coin regulated the rest), compared with the currencies of the Continent, most of which were much more degraded below their respective standards. That portion which was a real difference of exchange in our favour, and which therefore indicated a balance of debts in our favour, was owing to that credit which the merchants of England are enabled, by their great capitals and skill, to extend to the traders of almost all foreign countries. This appears to us a more correct explanation of the fact, than that which is suggested by Lord King. For the purposes, however, of his general argument, the fact alone is enough, that, in the present commercial relations of Britain, the real difference of exchange is almost permanently in our favour. This corroborates all the other arguments which have been

94

adduced to shew, that nothing but a derangement and depreciation of our currency can explain the appearance, continued since 1799, of an exchange against us.

We cannot permit ourselves to dismiss this work, without expressing our approbation, both of the style and of the temper in which it is written. So great perspicuity is not often attained, upon a subject in its nature intricate and abstruse; but it is still more rare, upon a subject connected with the topics of political difference, to preserve such entire candour. The calmness with which the argument is pursued, and the clearness with which it is stated, might render this pamphlet a model for similar publications. In almost all the general principles, that are collaterally introduced for the sake of illustration, the author is liberal and accurate; nor was an apology for these digressions in the smallest degree necessary. On the contrary, we have always thought, that such writers as undertake to inform the public mind upon measures of temporary interest, render themselves doubly and eminently useful, when they seize every opportunity of expounding those more extensive truths, which, though in possession of the learned, are not yet insinuated into popular conviction.—It is by innumerable repetitions of this sort, that an impression may at length be made, even on vulgar understandings, in favour of an enlightened policy; and the assent of the multitude habituated to the results of that genuine philosophy, whose high aim is to emancipate mankind from practical error, and to ameliorate their political condition.

Vol. V ([No. IX] Oct. 1804), Art. XV (pp. 190–208).
*An Act to Regulate the Importation and Exportation of Corn, and
the Bounties and Duties payable thereon. 30th July 1804.
44. of the King, cap. 109.*

*Cursory Observations on the Act for ascertaining the Bounties, and
for regulating the Exportation and Importation of Corn.* By a
Member of Parliament. London, Stockdale. 1804. pp. 16.

THAT part of the new Corn Law, in which the Legislature has
reverted to the system of bounties upon exportation, after
having in a great measure abandoned it for a period of thirty
years, appeared to us to bear so hard upon an established and
salutary doctrine in political economy, that we looked with eager-
ness for an opportunity of entering with our readers into a discussion of the measure. Hitherto, however, there has been no
publication upon the subject, except the statute itself; and we owe
too profound a reverence to parliamentary black-letter, to subject
it to the prophane license of Edinburgh criticism. One little tract,
the 'Cursory Observations,' was circulated in London, we understand, by one of those most respectable gentlemen with whom the
bill originated; but as it was not regularly published, it does not
fall within our reach. It was probably considered by the rest, as
the whole case they could make out; stated very briefly indeed,
but with neatness, great fairness, and all the strength that their
view of the argument was possessed of. In the course of our
Journal, our readers have been so much accustomed to find the
notice of a book nearly lost in dissertation, that they will perhaps
hardly be sensible of an innovation upon our plan by a dissertation
without any book for its text. If an apology however be necessary,
we must take it from the importance of the occasion. Opinions,
as well as compositions, have from the first been the object of our
humble endeavours to assist the public judgment; and we should
not have entered so minutely as we have often done into the examination of the latter, if we had not our eye always fixed on those
systems of useful knowledge which they contribute to form. We
shall therefore make no farther introduction to the following
investigation, except to mention, that the writers whom we have
principally in view, when we speak of advocates for the bounty,
are, Dr James Anderson, who, in his Letters on National Industry,
has given an elaborate argument in its defence; Mr Mackie of
Ormiston, in East Lothian, whose letters to Colonel Dirom display

96

much acuteness, as well as practical information; and Mr Malthus, the ingenious and enlightened author of the Essay on Population.*

The law which gave a bounty on the exportation of corn, will always be famous in the economical history of Great Britain, whatever may be the final opinion as to its merits. It originated under an administration, the splendour of whose measures is reflected even from their errors. And though, in framing that law, they were probably quite unconscious of the invention and design to which it has since been ascribed, yet, if we view it in a particular aspect, through the medium of those reasonings which have since been constructed in its favour, it may be made to appear a bold and original deviation, not only from the policy that had long prevailed, but from prejudices that are very natural on such subjects. In this light, accordingly, it appeared to the best writers and statesmen of England, throughout the first part of the last century: They mentioned it always with admiration, as an institution that had been planned in wisdom, and the success of which was complete;—to be ranked with the act of navigation, the laws for the woollen staple, or Queen Elizabeth's provision for the poor—an inseparable part of that peculiar system, to which England was indebted for her superiority over all other nations. These vague and confident praises of the bounty had long been established among the idioms of parliament, even before some circumstances in the later history of the corn-trade were attended to, which seemed to furnish a very plausible confirmation of them. The diminution of the average price, and the progressive increase of exports, within the period at the beginning of which the bounty had been instituted, presented no doubt a very deceitful coincidence; and, at a time when the analysis of national wealth was unknown, it was natural enough to believe, that the cause of these curious facts could be no other, but that remarkable law which just preceded their appearance. These sentiments, with regard to King William's corn-law, were adopted by our admirers upon the Continent. The bounty became a theme of panegyric in all their political treatises. Though a most artificial expedient, it was applauded even by the economists of France, in whose profound writings all devices were reprobated, that might check the spontaneous order of nature. In the mean time, opinions more consistent

---

* To this last gentleman, we owe many apologies for having delayed so long the account of his original and important work; and for anticipating, as in this article, the examination of a detached part of it. It is as well to confess at once, that the person, into whose hands it was put, has disappointed us, from indolence or other occupations, or a sense of the difficulty and extent of Mr Malthus's speculations. We have reason, however, to hope that it will make its appearance in our January Number.

with the tenor of their other speculations were spreading in this country, among well educated men of practice, as well as philosophical inquirers; and Parliament at last began to enforce some of those principles, which, many years before, had been expounded in the lectures of Adam Smith. The act of 1773, which was conducted through the House of Commons by Mr Burke, effected a virtual repeal of the bounty, though it retained the language, and seemed even to confirm the purposes of the former law, in compliance with those prejudices which it was easier to betray then to conquer. Dr Smith has said of this statute, what was said of the laws of Solon, that, though not the best in itself, it was perhaps the best which the interests and temper of the times would admit of. He probably bore in mind, when he used these expressions, the answer which Mr Burke had made to him, on being reproached for not effecting a thorough repeal, that it was the privilege of philosophers to conceive their diagrams in geometric accuracy: but the engineer must often impair the symmetry, as well as simplicity of his machine, in order to overcome the irregularities of friction and resistance. In the same strain, Dr Smith has likewise said of that statute, that it might perhaps in due time prepare the way for a better; and those who had most imbibed the spirit of his philosophy, acquiesced very confidently in this expectation. But, by another coincidence of circumstances, still more accidental perhaps than the former, the changes in the price of corn, and in the balance of the corn-trade, have been precisely reversed, since the repeal of the bounty, from changes which have taken place since the time of its enactment. Prices have risen, and the balance is turned against us. Those persons, who had been moved in favour of the bounty by the first part of this experience, as it seemed, could not help feeling the second to be irresistible: if the original trial furnished a probable conclusion, this converse of the experiment, yielding the same result, seemed to establish it to demonstration. The course of these facts appears, accordingly, to have made a great impression on several ingenious and well informed minds; the bounty has once more found advocates in some political writers of great merit, and in several statesmen, who are fortified by their general principles against artificial schemes of commercial police; and a statute has been passed, which, it is expected, will work all the miracles and blessings that are supposed to have been accomplished by the old law. Although we have long been satisfied about the wisdom of unimpaired freedom in every branch of the corn-trade, foreign as well as inland, we have been prompted, by our respect for those persons, and by the importance which is attached by them to the subject, to

98

examine very carefully the reasonings with which they recommend the revival of the bounty. In the course of this examination, we were led to perceive that Dr Smith's deductions are not perfectly correct; but in the practical conclusion, we were again brought to coincide with him, and with the statesmen who are understood to have framed, upon his principles, the act of 1773.

The earliest topics that were used in praise of the bounty, were, its great encouragement of British shipping, and the gold it brought home to pay the balance of exported corn. These have not been brought forward this time. So much we owe to the diffusion of knowledge. There are arguments and views of policy that were deemed irrefragable by the best understandings in the generation before the last, of which the refutation is now become even colloquial. It is a reflection that yields encouragement to the free scrutiny of other opinions, which appear no less susceptible of refutation. We are told, *first*, That a bounty, by forcing a production of corn greater than the annual consumption of the home-market, provides a reserve against years of deficient crop: *secondly*, That it secures an adequate profit to the farmer: *thirdly*, That it brings the prices of corn, which usually fluctuate so much, to a greater steadiness and uniformity: And, *lastly*, That it makes this uniform price rather lower than it otherwise would be. Upon these four propositions it may be observed, that the promised steadiness in the price of corn must be derived from that surplus of produce which is to be reserved in years of a bad crop. Now, this surplus of the average produce above the annual consumption, must be the result of an enlarged encouragement of tillage; and this encouragement, which operates by augmenting the profits of the farmer, must ultimately consist in an increase of the price of his commodity. So far, then, as the argument depends upon the first three of those alleged advantages, it resolves itself into this single proposition, that the bounty gives the farmer a real advance upon the price of his corn. When it is stated, in the fourth place, that it has likewise the effect of lowering the price of corn to the consumers, it is the money price only that can here with consistency be understood; a diminution of which is no doubt compatible with an advance of the real price. It appears, therefore, that when we examine what effects a bounty must have upon the commerce and growth of corn, our subject of investigation is precisely the effect of that bounty upon the real price, and upon the money-price of corn. Dr Smith, accordingly, who has decidedly pronounced an opinion very different from the foregoing, maintains it by propositions directly the reverse of those which we have enumerated:—that it can have no effect in equalizing

99

prices, because there is no surplus to be reserved in years of scarcity: that there can be no such surplus, because the bounty gives no additional encouragement to agriculture: that it can give no such encouragement, because it occasions no advance of the real price of corn: and, lastly, that its effect is to raise, not to lower, the average money-price of that commodity. In order to ascertain where the truth lies between such contradictory opinions, it will be necessary to trace, more minutely in detail than has hitherto been done, the influence which a bounty on corn must have upon its exchangeable value; whether that be expressed in money, or, in what is called the real price—the aggregate of other commodities that are purchased with money.

Let us suppose, in a country where the returns of the farmer are of course adequate, and no more than adequate, to replace his advances with a profit proportioned to the profits of other capital, that a bounty were granted out of the public revenue directly upon the *production* of bread corn. Its immediate effect would evidently be, to lower both the money-price and the real price to all purchasers in the home-market. A part of the old price, instead of being paid by the purchaser himself, would now be paid for him by the public; and while he paid so much less, the farmer would receive altogether the same sum as before. The farmer would no doubt be willing enough to keep up the market price to its original rate, that he might thus increase his receipts by the whole of the bounty. But the same power of competition, which had before adjusted his profits, would continue to adjust them to the same rate, by reducing his receipts from the private purchaser in proportion to his new receipts from the public. Notwithstanding this bounty, therefore, the profits of the farmer would, by the operation of the principle of competition, subside towards their former level. They would for some time, indeed, be kept from sinking quite down to this level, by the force of competition that would act in the opposite direction: For, in consequence of the real price of grain being lowered to the consumers, their power of purchasing this article would for the time be augmented, whether they had other commodities or their labour only to give in exchange; and thus the limits of the effective demand for grain would be widened, by a greater waste in the use and preparation of it for food, a nicer palate as to the quality, and ultimately by an increased number of consumers. The effect of such an increased demand for grain, proceeding from any other cause, must evidently be, to enhance a little its real price. The effect of this increased demand, proceeding from an artificial reduction of the real price, would be, to prevent that reduction from being wholly completed, to prevent the market

100

price from being lowered quite so much as by the whole amount of the bounty: The difference would be received by the farmer, in addition to the adjusted rate of his profits, and would of course operate as a new encouragement to tillage. It is evident, however, that this encouragement could last no longer than the increased demand in the home-market, from which it originated; and that could not subsist long, because, while the general circumstances of the nation remain the same, no reduction of the real price of corn can be permanent. The wages of the labouring consumers had been adjusted before, by the principle of competition, to a rate proportioned to those general circumstances; and the same principle would continue to adjust them again to that rate, by lowering the money-price of labour, and, through that, of other commodities, to the money-price of corn. Thus the whole effect of this bounty on production, would terminate in a reduction of the nominal or money-price. The real price would soon be raised, and the profit of the farmer soon lowered, to their former level; and the interval would speedily elapse, during which a new encouragement had been afforded to agriculture. At the close of that interval, both the absolute number of the people, and the gross annual produce, might be found a very little increased. The relative condition of the labouring orders, in respect of opulence and comforts, would be found unexchanged. And to defray the bounty, there would subsist a tax, probably very burdensome, certainly quite unnecessary; and it would subsist to no other purpose but to effect a preposterous inversion of the natural order of things.

If it should be deemed expedient to renew that sort of encouragement to tillage, which has now been described, it might no doubt be renewed by a fresh addition to the bounty; which would operate over again the same series of effects, leaving in the end the money-price still lower, and the tax still more burdensome: And such statesmen, as may have a predilection for artificial schemes of this sort, will easily see the superior artifice of meting out the bounty in small portions from time to time, in order that, with the smallest amount of bounty, there may be obtained the greatest number of these intervals of encouragement to agriculture.

If, on the other hand, it should be felt desirable to get rid of such a bounty as this, and to restore the commerce of grain to its natural course, such a step could not be taken without a great deal of temporary inconvenience; for that series of effects which took place after the enactment of the bounty, would be precisely inverted by its repeal. The sudden enhancement of the money-price would abridge, for the time, the wealth and comforts of the

101

labouring consumers; and the restriction of their demand, reducing the profits of farming below its natural rate, would for the time discourage agriculture: And this would continue until the advance of the money-price of corn communicated itself to the money-price of labour, and, through that, to the money-price of other commodities. It is unnecessary, for our present purpose, that we should attempt to trace any farther the consequences of a direct bounty upon *production*.

A bounty, granted out of the public revenue, upon the *exportation* only of corn, will operate according to the same principles; but, from the different manner in which the bounty is then applied, its effects will be considerably different. It will produce no *immediate* change of prices in the home-market. The national consumer will continue to pay what he did before, no part of this payment being made for him by the public: there will be no diminution to him of the real price of corn, consequently no enlargement of consumption and demand, and therefore no new encouragement on this side to agricultural investments. But every foreigner, who shall purchase part of the exported grain, will pay so much less for it, as the bounty amounts to, than he otherwise would have paid. Whether he will purchase any part of it or not, will of course depend upon this condition, that the price of the exported grain, reduced as it is to him by the bounty, is at the most not greater than the price of other grain in his market. Now, the price at which the exported grain could be sold in the foreign market, independently of a bounty, may either be equal, or less, or greater, compared with the price of other grain in that market. If equal, the bounty will enable the exporter to undersell the foreign dealer by the whole amount of that bounty. If less, he would be able, without a bounty, to undersell him by the whole difference of the prices; and the bounty will enable him to undersell by the sum of that difference and the bounty added together. If the price, at which the exported grain could be sold in the foreign market independently of a bounty, is greater than the price of other grain in that market; then, to enable the exporter to undersell the dealer in that other grain, the bounty must be more than sufficient to compensate the difference of the prices; and a bounty may no doubt be made large enough to do more than compensate that difference. In all these cases, too, it is to be observed, the exporter will actually undersell the foreign dealer by very nearly the whole difference by which he can afford to undersell him. He would be willing enough to do it by as small a portion of that difference as possible, in order that the remainder might be added to his profits; but the force of competition, as upon all other occasions, will

102

restrict his profits very nearly to the lowest rate at which he can afford to trade. They will not be brought quite down to this rate, however; the exporter will not be forced to undersell the foreign dealer by quite the whole difference by which he could afford to do it, in consequence of a competition that will act in the opposite direction. For, by the reduction of the real price to the foreign consumers, their effective demand will be enlarged; and this enlarged demand will prevent that reduction which the bounty has a tendency to effect, from being wholly completed. The difference will be received by the exporter in an addition to the adjusted rate of his profits; and, the extension of foreign demand being communicated to the home market, will raise at home both the price of corn and the profits of farming. By raising the profits of farming, it will operate as an encouragement to husbandry; by raising the price of corn to the consumers at home, it will diminish for the time their power of purchasing this necessary of life, and thus abridge their real wealth. It is evident, however, that this last effect must be temporary; the wages of the labouring consumers had been adjusted before by competition, and the same principle will adjust them again to the same rate, by raising the money-price of labour, and, through that, of other commodities, to the money-price of corn. The bounty upon exportation, therefore, will ultimately raise the money-price of corn in the home market; not directly, however, but through the medium of an extended demand in the foreign market, and a consequent enhancement of the real price at home: And this rise of its money-price, when it has once been communicated to other commodities, will of course become fixed.

This fixed advance of the money-price at home will necessarily affect the price at which the exported corn can afterwards be sold in the foreign market. It will of course diminish that difference, whatever it is, by which the exporter can undersell the dealer in foreign grain. That difference, however, may still be large enough, with the assistance of the bounty, to allow the exporter still to undersell that dealer; and to occasion, in the same manner as before, a farther extension of demand. This will be followed, as before, by a series of effects, ultimately terminating in a farther advance of the money-price at home: And this series will be constantly renewed, until the advance of that money-price becomes so high, as to cover the whole difference by which the exporter was before able to undersell other dealers abroad. By a new bounty, however, granted in addition to the former, a new range may be created for the repetition of another series of the same effects. But, whatever limit we suppose to the amount of the bounty, its complete and ultimate effect will always be found to be a corresponding rise of the money-price in the home market, both of corn, of labour, and of all commodities. In the interval that must each time elapse, before wages are equalized with each successive rise in the price of corn, there will be a certain degree of new encouragement held out to husbandry, and some diminution in the wealth and comfortable subsistence of the labouring consumers. That encouragement to husbandry will not be followed by any increase of the number of the people, because the additional production is excited by a foreign demand. And this diminution of the comforts of the labouring people, from being temporary, may become almost a permanent diminution, if the successive advances of the price of corn shall follow each other without interruption, and so keep always ahead of the successive advances in the wages of labour.

If it should be felt expedient to remove such a bounty as this upon exportation, and to restore the commerce and production of grain to their natural order, such a repeal would be attended with some temporary inconveniences. The sudden destruction of that part of the foreign demand, which had been forced by the bounty, would throw an excess upon the home market, and would reduce the profits of farming for a time below their actual and just rate. The national consumers would for a time be more easily and plentifully supplied; until, by the abstraction of capital from tillage, the supply of corn was once more accommodated to the real demand, and the profits of the farmer raised again to their natural rate.

If, in the preceding analysis, we have deduced with accuracy the operations of the principle of competition, a correction must be made in Dr Smith's argument upon the bounty. When we consider, indeed, the patient, circumspect, and comprehensive care which the reasonings of that great author almost always evince, and the hazard there is that, in a process of some length and intricacy, we may have overlooked one or more necessary steps, it is not without much diffidence that we presume to attempt such a correction. At present, however, he appears to us not to have completed this investigation with his usual success.

In the first two editions of his Inquiry, the form of the investigation is considerably different from that which appears in all the subsequent editions. In these, he states and answers separately two arguments that had been alleged by others in favour of the bounty—the extension of the foreign market, and the enhancement of price to the farmer. But in the first two editions of the work, there was no notice of any alleged extension of foreign

104

demand, but only of the single argument founded on the enhancement of price. By omitting all consideration of the foreign market,
he excluded that to which we have traced the operations of the
bounty as commencing in the first instance. In separating the
extension of the foreign market and the enhancement of price,
from each other, and treating them as quite distinct, he overlooked
that necessary connexion which we have endeavoured to point out
between them. In both cases, his error appears to have consisted
in too hastily assuming, from those whom he was about to refute,
that a bounty on exportation would occasion *immediately* a rise of
the money-price in the home-market: an assumption which
betrays itself explicitly, when he comes to speak of it as 'a very
moderate supposition, that a bounty of five shillings the quarter
upon exportation, may raise the price four shillings in the home-
market.' This assumption is evidently the foundation of his
separate answer to the alleged enhancement of price, in which his
general remarks are quite accurate, so far as they reach, but are
inadequate to the inference, which he founds upon them, that the
bounty can have no effect in raising the real price of corn; inasmuch as he has overlooked that *interval* which elapses, as we have
shown, between the enhancement of the money-price of corn, and
its communication to the money-price of labour and other commodities. In his separate answer to the alleged extension of
foreign demand, he does not expressly deny the fact, but affirms
that, in every particular year, this is at the expense of the home-
market, and endeavours to show that the bounty restrains also the
gradual extension of the home-market, by its enhancement of the
price. But in affirming that the quantity exported in every particular year, were it not for the bounty, would remain in the home
market, he evidently takes it for granted, that this quantity,
though there had been no bounty, would still have been grown:
Now, this is the very question upon which he undertakes to prove
his particular opinion. In endeavouring to show, that the enhancement of price, occasioned in the home-market by the bounty,
must restrain the population or the industry of the country, he
proceeds upon the above mentioned assumption, that the bounty
occasions an immediate rise of the money-price of corn, and
therefore must either reduce the subsistence of the labourers, or,
if wages rise, the ability of their employers to give them work. If
that rise of money-price, however, is consequent, as we have
shown, to an extension of demand in the foreign market, it will at
first increase the ability of those employers; and though it will
likewise reduce at first the subsistence of the labourers, their
wages must soon rise to their true rate; and this rise in the

money-price of labour will only reduce the ability of the employers to its former level.

If these criticisms on the reasoning of Dr Smith shall appear well founded to such of our readers as have bestowed on his work the study it merits, from all who are serving their apprenticeship to the science, or to the practice of commercial policy, they will at once perceive, that we have derived, out of the work itself, the means of correcting its imperfections.

Some of the errors, into which the advocates for the bounty have fallen, are more palpable, and proceed from an imperfect acquaintance with the fundamental principles of political economy.

In the *first* place, they have quite misunderstood Smith's important doctrine, that the variations of the money-price of corn are communicated ultimately to that of labour and other commodities. He has not perhaps stated this general truth, nor deduced the reasoning by which we are led to it, in a form perfectly unexceptionable; but his application of it to the operations of the bounty is quite legitimate. They have insisted, some of them at great length, that the price of commodities and labour is liable to be affected by many other circumstances, besides the price of corn. This is unquestionably true; but is surely not incompatible with Dr Smith's proposition, which, so far as it enters into his reasonings about the bounty, goes no farther than to assert, that every change it may occasion in the money-price of corn will communicate itself, first to the money-wages of labour, and, through them, to the money-price of all other articles; and that thus the real price of corn will be maintained the same, notwithstanding a nominal variation. Without a just apprehension of this fundamental truth, it is impossible to reason with accuracy upon the subject.

In the *second* place, they seem very imperfectly aware of the manner in which the principle of competition operates upon profits, and upon exchangeable value. And on this account, many of the remarks, which they have made, are inconsistent as well as unfounded. They have uniformly supposed, as Smith appears likewise to have done, that the sum of the bounty is immediately added to the former money-price even in the home market: at the same time, they contend that the average price in that market will be lowered. It is their opinion, that the real price of corn will upon the whole be rendered cheaper to the consumers, and that the same real price will be maintained permanently higher to the farmer; though these two positions are in direct terms contradictory of each other. When Mr Malthus, who is by far the most intelligent advocate for the bounty, observes that 'it lowered greatly the price of corn, by producing a growth considerably above the wants of the actual population,' he evidently forgets, that a greater growth can only be occasioned by a greater demand, which will always be adjusted to that, and, keeping the supply and the demand always in the same ratio, will in other words keep the price always at the same rate. And when this writer speaks of 'the experienced difficulty of lowering wages when once they have been raised,' he seems to have forgotten, for a moment, that very part of the great principle of competition upon which his own re-searches have thrown so much light; and, in fixing his eye upon an irregular movement at some part of the large machine, to have quitted his steady view of that uniform motion in which all the retarding and accelerating forces are found to have balanced one another. But the advocates for the bounty have betrayed a much less pardonable inattention to the necessary action of this principle of competition, when they conceive, as some of very high authority* have done, that the average price of grain in the home-market may be so low as not to yield a 'fair and reasonable' profit to the grower. We shall afterwards point out the share which this very erroneous prejudice may be supposed to have had, in recommend-ing the late legislative attempt: but it would be endless to submit, at this time of day, to the formal refutation of an error so palpable and so antiquated. We shall notice only one mistake more, into which the theoretical writers appear to have fallen. Both Dr Smith and his antagonists have pronounced, that, in years of extraordinary abundance, the bounty will prevent the money-price of corn in the home market from falling quite so low as it would fall if there were no bounty. In this position, Smith is quite consistent at least with himself, because he uniformly maintains that the bounty can have no effect in rendering the annual produce larger than it otherwise would be. But the same consistency can-not be allowed to those, who both assert this position, and assume that the bounty does increase the produce, and occasions a surplus growth above the annual consumption. For this surplus, it is to be observed, will, in a year of extraordinary abundance, partake of the extraordinary increase; so that, over and above the usual home supply, there will in such a year be reaped not only the extraordinary increase upon that supply, together with the usual surplus for exportation, but likewise the extraordinary increase upon that surplus. Of these four portions of the crop, therefore, not only the second, but the fourth also, will be thrown as an excess upon the home market; and the price in that market will

* Reports of the Committee of the House of Commons respecting the Corn-Trade, ordered to be printed 14th May and 14th June 1804.

consequently be lowered much more by the whole of this excess, than it would have been by the former part of it alone.

In the result, therefore, our idea of the operations of a bounty upon export differs a good deal from both the opinions which were stated at the outset of this investigation. We conceive that it may, in a particular manner, afford some temporary encouragement to tillage; and thus, to a certain degree, force the production of a surplus, which may be reserved for the home market in deficient years. By preventing, in those years, the temporary price from rising so high as it otherwise would, it may be considered as restraining a little on one side the occasional fluctuations of the price of corn; but, by overstocking the home market in plentiful years still more than it otherwise would be overstocked, it must be considered as giving a still greater range to the fluctuation of the temporary price on the other side. Whether or not it approximates one extreme point of variation more or less towards the ordinary price, than it removes the other, and whether or not it thus contracts or extends the whole range of occasional variation, is a question which it might be difficult to solve, but which is probably of greater curiosity than importance. While this is the influence of the bounty upon the temporary changes of real price, its effects, we conceive, upon the nominal price of corn, is to raise and keep it higher than it otherwise would be.

If that sort of encouragement to tillage, which we have here admitted, should be deemed a sufficient benefit to recommend to a great nation the establishment of a bounty, it must still be remembered that, though it may indirectly secure a more certain supply of corn, it necessarily retards, upon the whole, the growth of national opulence and industry. It forces a part of the national capital into a branch of trade, which is necessarily a losing one, and which does not return the whole of the capital that is employed in it. Defence, however, it has been said, is of more importance than opulence:* and an independent supply of subsistence lies at the foundation of the means of defence. The general observation is undeniable. The truths of political economy form but a class among the principles of administration, and in their practical application must often be limited by higher maxims of state, to which in theory too they are held subordinate, as being less general. Yet, unless this subordination is finely and truly felt, the limit may be placed very injudiciously; and we may be summoned to deviate from general rules, whenever a statesman takes fright at a temporary inconvenience, or is captivated with some specious project of a remedy. The wisdom which would become

* Wealth of Nations, II. 195.

this mature age of English policy, is of more simple arrangements, as well as firmer to its purpose. A case should be made out of controuling necessity, and of a result clearly overbalancing, by the advantage, all disadvantages that may be concomitant. After estimating to its full amount the possible benefit to be derived from such an artificial contrivance as the bounty, we must not only weigh, against that, both the immediate sacrifice and all the subsequent disadvantages, but we ought likewise to consider whether the very benefit proposed, at least in one point of view, might not be better obtained in another way—as by the removal of any existing impediments to cultivation, to the free commerce of land, the free employment of capital, or the free transference of labour. There is an immediate sacrifice in forcing the national capital into a branch of trade in which part of it is absolutely lost; for the whole sum granted in bounties, together with the expences of collecting the tax by which they are defrayed, is a part of the national capital thrown into that trade without any return. There is some disadvantage, in that constant diminution of the real wages of labour, which is occasioned by the progressive rise of the price of corn in the home market. Very considerable disadvantages are incurred, from the constant enhancement of the money price of labour and all other commodities, both in the depreciation of fixed pecuniary returns, and in the injury to domestic manufactures in their competition against foreign industry. But the greatest disadvantage, perhaps, of all, consists in the uncertainty and derangements to which interferences of law subject the capital that is vested in the trade of grain, and the obstacle which these oppose to the free enlargement and consolidation of that most important system of commerce. On the other hand, the encouragement, such as it is, which any assigned bounty will give to husbandry, must expire after a short interval—as soon as the money price of corn in the home market has risen, and it cannot fail to rise, so high as to cover the whole advantage, which the bounty had originally given to the exporter in his sales abroad: and the whole encouragement, or stimulus, which, even during this interval, the bounty can give to agriculture, will be found to be very slight, if we consider the manner in which this stimulus is formed; and that it consists, not, as it has hitherto been represented, in the addition of the whole bounty to the farmer's price, but in that small addition to his price, which is occasioned from time to time by the gradual extension of foreign demand. It may be important, likewise, with reference to the present circumstances of this country, to remark, that, when the average price of corn at home is greater than that of the foreign market, the interval of encouragement to tillage, under the same bounty, will be shorter than in the other two cases, and the whole disadvantage of high money-prices will be sooner brought to its greatest height.

The present circumstances of the country, with respect to its agricultural produce, have excited a very unnecessary alarm among some of our legislators as well as political writers. It is affirmed, that as, in years of scarcity, we have been dependent on very large importations from abroad, we are even in ordinary years dependent upon importation for a certain portion of our necessary supply. If the fact be so, of which there is not yet full proof in possession of the public, we can discover no reason why it should be considered as more than a temporary and slight inconvenience. A bounty upon exportation, at any rate, and the prohibition of importations, do not seem to form the most reasonable sort of remedy for sych a state of things, or one that is very likely to prove successful. An entire freedom of importation, combined with a bounty upon production augmented from time to time, might have appeared at least a more plausible proposal. But it is evident that all such schemes must be nugatory, compared with the remedy which a supply, too narrow for the actual demand, provides for itself. The demand in the home market is at all times by far the most powerful, generally the sole, encouragement to cultivation; and its power must be increased immensely, when circumstances force on the demand still more rapidly than the supply can be augmented. In the present circumstances of Great Britain, the law surely can add nothing to the permanent encouragement of agriculture, though there are a few impediments which it might remove. Nothing can be more unfounded than the fears which some advocates for the bounty have expressed, that England may cease to be an independent agricultural nation; except the lamentations, which others have indulged over the actual decline of its husbandry since the fatal statute of the year 1773. They must have lost all trust in their own memory, as well as the evidence of their senses, who can doubt for an instant, that from year to year of this period the husbandmen of Britain have extended their capital, their skill, and their produce. The commerce and the manufactures of the island conceal in some measure its agricultural grandeur; of which we may not perhaps obtain a full view, unless this splendid superstructure of our present prosperity, mouldering away from the fragility of the materials, or shattered by external violence, shall expose the strength and extent of the base on which it rested. Like Lombardy, and Tuscany and Flanders, England would be left rich and orderly even in ruin; and would be resorted to, for the lessons of her ancient husbandry, by such nations as

110

might then be accumulating from commerce the resources of agricultural improvement. In the mean time, the growth of our population, and the distribution of wealth among the industrious classes, accelerated at a rate with which our agriculture cannot keep pace, instead of showing symptoms of decay, form an unprecedented case of rapid progression; favoured a little by an accidental conjuncture in the political situation of neighbouring states, but originating in the condition of our national opulence itself. It is a fact, indeed, from which the inference to the present argument seems irresistible—although a full explanation of it is not yet furnished by our knowledge of general principles. For the different employments of national capital, and the progress in which they naturally succeed each other, or alternate, form a subject on which we are not yet in possession of a complete theory; though a beautiful sketch was drawn by Dr Smith,* to which many original remarks have been added by Mr Brougham in his work upon Colonial Policy, and some happy illustrations by Lord Lauderdale in the last chapter of his late publication. It is a subject, the farther investigation of which we earnestly recommend to our speculative readers, as it would throw light on some of the most important points of the wealth and economy of nations. Such an investigation, we have little doubt, would prove that the deficiency of domestic produce, which may take place in a great agricultural country from an accelerated diffusion of wealth among the people, can only be temporary, though it may occasionally recur; and ought to be considered as indicating, in the clearest manner, the velocity of that natural current, which the regulations of law may check, but never can impel. A careful collection of some circumstances in the history of different nations, such as have always been most neglected by historians, would curiously show, that similar oscillations in the balance of the trade of provisions, have often accompanied the most steady progress of accumulating wealth. Lord Bacon, we remember, in some of his political treatises, has more than once found occasion to remark, that 'whereas England was wont to be fed by other countries from the east, it sufficeth now to feed other countries;' and that 'the good yields of corn, together with some toleration of rent, hath enticed men to break up more ground, than all the penal laws, for that purpose made and enacted, could ever by compulsion effect.'†

The bounty seems likewise to have recommended itself to some

* From the beginning of the Fifth Chapter of the Second Book, to the end of the Third Book.
† See his Advice to Villiers, and the Observations on a Libel.

of its admirers, by that air of ingenious contrivance which they fancy that they perceive in it. The very simple expedient, of paying a few shillings at the custom-house, is to secure such a surplus of annual produce as will equalize the variation of value, and establish even a remedy against the natural inequality of the seasons. The bounty, it would seem, being attached to this irregular system of supply and prices, is to perform the functions of what mechanicians call a fly, attached to an engine in which the opposite pressures are apt to become unequal. It is to accumulate a surplus of produce, by which an occasional deficiency shall be supplied; and it is to act as a regulator of the price, against the circumstances that tend to enhance or to depress it. If it can be said to do all this, it may be said to do something more; 'to repress,' as Mr Malthus has inferred, 'to repress the principle of population a little in years of plenty, and to encourage it comparatively in years of scarcity; regulating, in this manner, the population more equally, according to that quantity of subsistence which can permanently be supplied.'* For ourselves, we confess, that all this appearance of device and project would raise a presumption against the bounty, if we were still unprovided with a more legitimate conviction. In the real machinery of the arts, human ingenuity only proceeds to render less imperfect its own designs; but the mechanism of commerce and circulation proceeds from another hand; and we can only disorder the scheme when we presume to touch it. That can rarely be wisdom for one great state, which may not permanently be followed by all. All cannot, by adopting the bounty, secure to each an export of corn; and the single nation that stoops from the plain high maxims of policy to so paltry an artifice, will ultimately be convinced that not even a paltry advantage can be gained. The balance of this trade cannot long be very great to any nation; and it will naturally be possessed by that one, whose capital and skill are in a condition to furnish the additional supplies most advantageously to all. In this condition, if the exportation is free, it will hold the balance, without requiring the aid of a bounty; nor can a bounty give it the balance, if it is not in that condition. In one instance, indeed, it has happened, that a bounty was in force while a particular nation was in this condition; and the possession of the balance was ascribed, not to the condition, but to the bounty. A bounty upon exportation, it is to be observed, implies, to a certain length, a free exportation; and the real consequences of that freedom are very apt to be ascribed to the bounty.

We are afraid, however, that in the late relapse of our Legislature

* P. 457.

to the old exploded system, some effect is to be imputed to an error of a much coarser fabric than either this project about a surplus, or the apprehensions of a national deficiency. Without the aid of the new statute, it has been said, the farmer cannot be sure of obtaining, even in the home market, a 'fair and reasonable profit.' If he cannot, without this statute, secure that profit, he has but little chance of it with all its assistance. How so gross a prejudice could be listened to again, after all that people have been taught, it becomes necessary to explain. Like other sorts of trade, that of the farmer is liable occasionally to the spirit of overtrading, if profits for a time have happened to be greater than ordinary. The late years of dearth and most extraordinary price, rendered the profits of farming, for the time, much greater than ordinary; and the consequence appears to have been, a pretty free indulgence of the disposition to trade too much, and to enter into projects disproportioned to the capital that would immediately be invested. In many instances, where farmers came to make a new agreement about rent, they reckoned too confidently upon the continuance of prices which they ought to have considered as unusual; and made the estimate of their future returns too much upon the recent rate of profit, and not upon an average sufficiently and reasonably large. Like other improvident speculators, they were, of course, to suffer for their want of foresight, as soon as prices and profit returned to their ordinary rate. The loss suffered by the improvident, is 'the fair and reasonable,' as well as the unavoidable, consequence of imprudence; of which it is at once the punishment and the preventive. The number of those who overtraded in this manner, was of course small, compared with the whole number of farmers; but that is no reason why their voice should not be loudest, when the majority have no interest in contradicting them. As a few merchants, whose credit is exhausted, and who can get no money to borrow, persuade, not themselves only, but all the world, that there is too little money in the country, the farmers, to whom it is difficult to make good their imprudent engagements, find it almost as easy to persuade other persons as themselves, that prices are a great deal too low. Their landlords, in particular, are not the persons most likely to discover that prices are not too low, but rents a little too high: and they may honestly find it somewhat difficult to be convinced that the embarrassment of their tenants is owing to that local cause, and not to something that affects the general condition of the country. The country gentlemen, accordingly, upon the recent occasion, spoke out with that explicit plainness from which they seldom deviate, even when they most mislead the public councils. In the pamphlet whose title we have

113

prefixed to the present article, it is said, that 'times, unfortunate in other respects, impressed on tillage a renovated vigour; a vigour which the principles of this act, and these alone, are able to sustain.' And in the second Report* of the Committee of the House of Commons, the same acknowledgement is still more express—

'It appears to your Committee, that the price of corn, from 1791 to the harvest of 1803, has been very irregular; but, upon an average, increased in a great degree by the years of scarcity, has in general yielded a fair profit to the grower. The usual high prices, however, have had the effect of stimulating industry, and bringing into cultivation large tracts of waste land; which, combined with the two last productive seasons, and other causes, have occasioned such a depression in the value of grain, as it is feared will greatly tend to the discouragement of agriculture, unless maintained by the support of Parliament.'

One might imagine that the framers of this reasoning have proceeded upon the supposition of a *cast* of farmers, whose numbers and whose capitals do not admit, or ought not to be suffered to admit, of being diminished by the operation of the principle of competition. The success of such topics almost carries one back (which is not the effect of many other appearances at present) from the years of the nineteenth century to the times of the old country party. But the success might not perhaps have been equally great, if the Master of the State had already been securely fixed upon that vantage ground, from which he may now dictate a policy more congenial to his former system. Amidst the arrangements of foreign policy and war which may be supposed to absorb his mind, the humble and less precarious plans of domestic legislation may be forgotten. But the minister who tampers, for a present purpose, with his own maxims, and indulges individuals in their frivolous fondness for making laws, instead of opposing, to temporary interests, the spirit of a general policy, cannot be true, either to his own fame, or to the lasting prosperity of Britain.

* Ordered to be printed, 14th June 1804.

Vol. VII ([No. XIII] Oct. 1805), Art. XIII (pp. 185–202).
Observations on the Present State of the Highlands of Scotland;
with a View of the Causes and probable Consequences of Emigra-
tion. By the Earl of Selkirk. Longman & Co. London. And
Constable & Co. Edinburgh. 8vo. pp. 224. App. pp. lvi.

IN one of the articles of our First Number, we expressed a wish
that some writer would afford us a proper opportunity of laying
before our readers the true history of the emigrations from the
Highlands, as connected with the improvements of landed property, and of explaining, at the same time, the policy which an
enlightened government should pursue with respect to such emigrations. Our wish is gratified to its full extent by this publication,
in which Lord Selkirk has undertaken both these subjects, and
executed them in a manner so entirely agreeable to the views
which we have always entertained, that we never could have
accomplished our original design nearly so well, as we shall now
do, by extracting the substance of the present work.

Besides an accurate description of the nature and causes of the
emigration, and a just explanation of the principles which ought to
guide the opinion of Government, there is another portion of the
book, which will be thought by many of our readers more enter-
taining than even the general disquisitions;—an account of the
colony of Highland Emigrants, founded by Lord Selkirk on Prince
Edward's Island, near the coast of Nova Scotia. The circumstances are very pleasing, to which he assigns the origin of this
expedition, and the composition of his book. Without any local
connexion with the Highlands, he was led, very early in life, to
take a warm interest in the fate of his countrymen in that part of
the kingdom. During the course of his academical studies, his
curiosity was strongly excited by the representations he heard of
the ancient state of society, and the striking peculiarity of manners
still remaining among them; and, in the year 1792, he undertook
an extensive tour through their wild region, and explored many of
its remotest and most secluded vallies. In the course of this expedition, he ascertained several of the leading facts on which the
reasonings of his work are founded; in particular, that emigration
was an unavoidable result of the general state of the country,
arising from causes above all control, and in itself essential to the
tranquillity and permanent welfare of the kingdom. In consequence
of this persuasion, that there was no reasonable hope of preventing emigration, he was led to direct his inquiries to the
destination of the various emigrants. He learned, that the

Highlanders were dispersing to a variety of situations in a foreign land, where they were lost, not only to their native country, but to themselves as a separate people. Admiring many generous and manly features in their character, he could not observe without regret, the rapid decline of their genuine manners, to which the circumstances of the country seemed inevitably to lead. He thought, however, that a portion of the ancient spirit might be preserved, even in the New World, by collecting the emigrants together in some part of our own colonies: there they would prove a benefit to the mother country; and those peculiarities of customs and language, might still be retained, which they are themselves so reluctant to give up, and which are perhaps intimately connected with many of their most striking and characteristic virtues. We shall mention, in the sequel of our abstract, the measures which Lord Selkirk took to carry these benevolent motives into effect: his present publication has grown out of the statements which he submitted to the Colonial Department of Government, in explanation of his views.

It is a book which will by no means perish with the local prejudices which it was designed to remove. It has other claims to a permanent reputation and utility. Not only will it preserve a better picture, than has been drawn by any other hand, of a peculiar state of society and manners, highly interesting to the historian; but it forms a large contribution, to the theory of political economy, of most satisfactory deductions and general conclusions. It would be no slight service of itself, however, to extinguish ignorant declamations against the emigrants, and to correct that mistaken spirit of regulation which professes to force comforts upon them against their wish: and we have seldom read any composition so well qualified to gain over the public mind from error, both by the perspicuous extent of its evidence and reasonings, and by the candid, unassuming, and very practical tone in which they are proposed. We hasten, therefore, to draw out an analysis of its principal contents for the instruction of our readers; and shall content ourselves with remarking, once for all, that Lord Selkirk's arrangement, and style of language, are so clear, and the latter so suitable in every respect to the subject, that we shall seldom deviate from either, except when we are anxious to be more concise than it would be proper for him to have been.

I. Not more than sixty years ago, the state of society in the Highlands of Scotland was very similar to that of England before the Norman conquest. Government had not yet extended its regular authority over these mountains, where the chieftains lived in a barbarous independence, surrounded by vassals and retainers.

116

The law was too feeble to afford protection, amidst the violence of feudal warfare and plunder; and every proprietor of land depended, for his safety and his consequence, on a numerous train of followers. To this consideration, every advantage of pecuniary interest was inferior; he reckoned the value of his estate, not by the rent, but by the number of men it could send into the field: the rent, in fact, was paid, not in money, but in military services. The small rental of the estates forfeited in the two rebellions of the last century has, accordingly, been often remarked with surprise; 'Poor twelve thousand *per annum*' (says Pennant) 'nearly subverted the constitution of these kingdoms:' but, with this narrow income, proprietors of middling rank brought into the field three, four, or five hundred men. Were the present high rents of the same estates to be all laid out in employing labourers, the number of these would not be very different from that of the clans that came from them in arms. There are various documents still extant, which ascertain the number of men that particular chiefs could bring out; and, on comparing them with the present value of their estates, the proportion appears to be, in general, between 10*l.* and 15*l.* for every man: This sum is not far from the yearly expense of a farm servant at the rate now current in the North of Scotland.

In this state of things, a system of occupancy was spread over the Highlands, which, though now disappearing, remained entire for some time after the last rebellion, and may still be found in many considerable districts. Every proprietor reduced his farms into as small portions as possible; and his design was seconded by the natural inclinations of his people. The state of the country left a father no means of providing for his sons, but by dividing his farm; and where two families could be placed upon the land instead of one, the chief acquired a new tenant and a new soldier. Hence every spot was occupied by as many families as its produce could maintain; and the ground was subdivided into very small possessions. The farms of the common tenantry, or *small tenants*, are held (we may still speak in the present tense) by joint occupiers, usually six or eight, sometimes many more; and form a sort of hamlets or petty townships, called, in the low country dialect, *touns*, and, in the Gaelic language, *bailé*. The shares of these partners are of course liable to become unequal, by subdivision or accumulation. The farm is generally a portion of a valley, to which is annexed a tract of mountain pasture, stretching some miles. The habitations are collected in a village, upon the best part of the arable land. This is sometimes cultivated in common, but more usually distributed among the tenants, in proportion to their shares; seldom, however, in a permanent manner, but from

117

year to year. The produce of the tillage land rarely affords a superfluity above the maintenance of the tenants and their families. Their riches consist of cattle, chiefly breeding cows, and the young stock produced from them, which are maintained on the farm till of a proper age for the market; and, by the sale of these, the tenants are enabled to pay their rent. The number which each farm or *toun* is capable of maintaining, is ascertained by usage, and may be, in general, from 30 to 80 cows, besides other cattle. The total amount is divided among the occupiers, according to their respective shares, no one being allowed to keep more than his regulated proportion. Besides these joint occupiers, there are *tacksmen* holding entire farms, who are of the rank of gentry, and trace their origin to some ancient proprietor of the estate, who had granted the farm as a provision for one of the younger branches of his family. These, formerly, were nearly upon the same footing as proprietors; they were the officers who, under the chief, commanded in the military expeditions of the clan. A part of their farm is sufficient to supply their own families; and they divide the rest among a number of subtenants or *cotters*, who are bound to perform a certain quantity of labour upon the farm, instead of paying rent for their small portion of land, and are allowed to pasture their cows along with the cattle of the farm. Cotters are to be found, likewise, upon the farms of the small tenants; two or three being generally employed, as servants to the partnership, for herding the cattle. There are also a few people who exercise the trades of blacksmiths, weavers, taylors, shoemakers, &c. and bargain with one or other of the tenants for a portion of his land. For, whatever additional employment a man may follow, he must always occupy a small spot of land, to raise provisions for himself and his family: if he cannot procure such a possession, he cannot live in the country. There is no such person known in the Highlands, as an independent labourer.

Such a state of property and manners, where every inhabitant is connected with land, where almost all its produce is consumed upon the spot, and where there is no distinct separation of employments, has been preserved nearly entire to this day. While the other districts of the island were brought, one after another, within the arrangement of one complex system of production and commerce, the Highlands were cut off from all the contagion of industrious enterprize, by the same rocky barrier which detached them from the jurisdiction of justice and law. Those barriers were at length broken down, by the measures which were adopted after the suppression of the rebellion in 1745: the country was disarmed; it was intersected by military roads; a force, sufficient to command it, was stationed at all the principal passes; and thus the authority of regular government was completely established. The chiefs ceased to be petty monarchs; the services of their followers were no longer requisite for defence, or useful in plunder: and when thus reduced to the same situation with proprietors in other parts of the kingdom, they soon discovered that their rents were far below the real value of their lands. The influence of old habits, of feudal vanity, and of attachment to their vassals, long prevailed over the prospect of pecuniary profit; but the more necessitous or less generous set the example: a generation has succeeded, educated under other circumstances; and the Highland proprietors have now no more scruple, than those of any other part of the kingdom, in turning their estates to the best advantage. Had these estates been susceptible of cultivation under a favourable climate, the proprietors would have found it their interest to clear them of the superfluous population, and to throw their multiplicity of small farms together into the hands of one or two farmers of capital and skill; agreeably to the remark of Dr Adam Smith, 'that the diminution of cottagers, and other small occupiers of land, has, in every part of Europe, been the immediate forerunner of improvement and better cultivation.' But the climate of the Highlands is adverse to the production of grain; and that mountainous region contains few mines that can attract knots of population, and is entirely destitute of coals, which might have encouraged the settlement of manufactures. In such a district, the most profitable employment of land is universally found to be the rearing of young cattle and sheep, which, at a proper age, are bought by farmers in more fertile countries, and fattened for the butcher. A few tracts in the north are adapted for the pasturing of black cattle; but sheep-farming must prevail over the range of mountains. The rapid and continual progress which this system is making, the great profits that have been reaped, and the increased rate of rents, sufficiently prove how well it is adapted to the natural circumstances of the Highlands. The few spots among the mountains that are susceptible of cultivation, are found to be more advantageously kept in grass, to afford a reserve of pasture and shelter to the flocks during the extreme rigour of winter. A few adventurous individuals, who had been accustomed to sheep-farming in the south of Scotland, saw the vast field which was opened in the Highlands to their capital and enterprize. The large profits, which soon rewarded their penetration and perseverance, as in the case of all those who introduce new and successful modes of agriculture, soon attracted others, and demonstrated to the proprietors themselves the benefits they might earn under this most suitable plan of management.

Such a revolution, however, in the system of landed property, must be accompanied by an entire change in the distribution of the inhabitants. The population must be cast into a new form. The class of small tenants will gradually disappear; the distinction will at length be marked out, between the station of farmer and that of labourer; and as many of the cotters as can remain in the country, will gradually fall into the various fixed employments that are necessary in the business of an extended farm. But the whole population on each farm will ultimately be reduced to the number of families that are absolutely required for this necessary business. A few shepherds with their dogs, will be sufficient for all the work of many an extensive range. The produce will no longer be consumed wholly upon the spot, in affording a scanty subsistence to an indolent contented tribe; but will supply, at a distance, the wasteful luxury of industrious crowds.

During the operation of this change, and the temporary derangement it occasions, much individual distress will unavoidably be suffered. A great part of the inhabitants must, in one way or another, seek for means of livelihood totally different from those on which they have hitherto depended. But the country affords no means of living, without a possession of land; they must look for resources, therefore, where there is a prospect of employment, and must bring their mind to the resolution of removing at least from their native spot. Two prospects present themselves. In the Low Country of Scotland, the wages of manufacturing labour; in America, the easy acquisition of land in absolute property. Of these alternatives, it is easy to perceive which will best suit the inclination and habits of the Highlander. Each of these two changes would exact very nearly the same effort over the natural affections of the mind; but the execution of the latter plan must be attended with more expense than the other. It will be practicable, therefore, to those only who can afford this expense. The class of cotters may be distinguished, in this respect, from that of small tenants: though the line is not always exactly defined, some very opulent cotters being as well provided as the lowest of the tenants, yet there is a great difference, generally speaking, in the amount of their respective property, and consequently in the views which they entertain after being dispossessed of their land. The cotters have seldom property enough for the necessary expenses of emigration; and few of them have ever been able to emigrate: they have, in general, removed into the manufacturing districts of the Low Country of Scotland. But the population of the Highlands

120

was composed, in a very large proportion, of the small tenants; and all of these are possessed of something that might be denominated capital. Most of them live much more wretchedly, as to habitation and diet, than the labourers who earn daily wages in other parts of the island; but they have property of greater value. A farmer of about thirty acres of arable land has perhaps property to the amount of about one hundred and sixteen pounds Sterling, while the annual consumption of provisions for his family and servants does not exceed fifteen pounds. In general, the small tenant, according to his share of the farm, has from three or four, to six or eight cows, with the proportionate number of young cattle; he has horses also, a few small sheep, implements of agriculture, and various household articles. By disposing of all this stock, especially if the price of cattle happens to be high, he is enabled to embark in undertakings which cannot be thought of by the cotter, and which are not within the reach of the peasantry, even in the more improved and richer parts of the island.

To those who can thus afford the expenses of the passage and first settlement, the low price of land in America presents the prospect of speedily attaining a situation and mode of life similar to that in which all their habits have been formed. Accustomed to possess land, to derive from it all the comforts they enjoy, to transmit their possessions from father to son, and to cherish all the prejudices of hereditary transmission, they most naturally consider themselves as born to a landed rank, and can form no idea of happiness separate from such a possession. Contrasted with such a situation, that of a day-labourer in a manufacturing town appears contemptible and degrading. It would be a painful change, also, to the practice of sedentary continued labour, from that life of irregular exertions, and long intervals of indolence in which the Highlander enjoys almost the freedom of a savage. It is but a temporary effort that is demanded of him, to carry his family across the Atlantic; and whether he prefers this, or emigrates down into the Low Country of Scotland, he is forced to a change; his habits are broken; he must form himself to a new mode of life. Whether he shall enter upon one to which all his feelings are repugnant, or by a better exertion of courage, economy, and foresight, regain a prouder and more secure independence, is an alternative in which his choice will assuredly be determined by his ability. By their ability or inability to afford the expenses of their passage to America, the choice of the Highlanders, with a very few exceptions, has been entirely regulated. Even among those whose poverty forced them to go at first into the manufacturing towns, some of the most remarkable exertions of industry have been

121

prompted, only by the desire of accumulating as much money as might enable them to join their friends beyond the Atlantic.

Thus it appears, that in the subversion of the feudal economy, and the gradual extension of the commercial system over that quarter of the island, emigration forms a necessary part of the general change. The race of cotters, after filling up the demand for menial labour that is still required under the new arrangement, are withdrawn into the manufacturing districts. A few of the small tenants, who, with some amount of capital, combine industry and good management, take a part in this new system, and grow up into farmers on a greater scale; but the rest of this class will be gradually and entirely drained off by emigration. And, in this manner, the commercial form of property and population will at length be fully established over the Highlands; and the peasantry placed in that relative station, which is best adapted to the purposes of national wealth. Emigration, it must always be recollected, is one of the results or necessary conditions of this change, and which cannot be abstracted from its other concomitant effects.

There is some reason to believe, that while the emigrations operate this necessary change in the character and composition of the population, they do not ultimately reduce the numbers, even in the Highlands. A place, for example, has been pointed out upon the west coast by Mr Irvine, which, in 1790, contained 1900 inhabitants, of whom 500 emigrated the same year to America; in 1801, the same spot contained 1967, though it had furnished 87 men for the army and navy, and not a single stranger had settled in it. There is no part of the Highlands where the people have so strong a spirit of emigration as in Long Island; yet a population of 5268, at the time of Dr Webster's survey in the year 1755, was found increased to 8308 at the time of Sir John Sinclair's survey in 1792. Emigrations from the Isle of Sky to North Carolina, have continued to a great amount since the year 1770; to the amount of 4000, it has been computed, prior to the year 1791, besides an equal number that has come into the low country: in 1755, this island contained 11,252, inhabitants; and in 1792, it contained 14,470. That emigration does not necessarily imply a permanent diminution of local numbers, but, on the contrary, may leave resources for a larger increase of a different sort of inhabitants, will be admitted by all those who have examined the theory of population.

Even if the depopulation of the Highlands were proved, we ought to judge of the whole effect, by taking the whole kingdom into view. The produce raised upon the mountains under the grazing system, is assuredly not less than it was formerly, though

122

it is not consumed upon the spot. There cannot be a doubt, indeed, that it is greatly augmented under the improved management. The diminution of tillage must be deducted from the whole increase of pasturage produce; but the tillage that is retained is of a much superior kind; and the introduction of pasture and the breeding system upon the mountains, will leave free, for an extended tillage, those arable plains of the south, which have been hitherto kept in grass for that purpose. The various climates, and all the different levels of the island, are thus formed into one connected plan of rural economy, distributing its produce through the whole family of the people.

Among the supposed effects of emigration, none has been more universally lamented than the loss of that valuable supply of soldiers which the public service has hitherto derived from the Highlands. But, independently altogether of emigration, the circumstances no longer exist which rendered the Highlands such a nursery of soldiers. Wherever the system of numerous dependants and very low rents was still adhered to, the chieftain had a double hold of the services of his tenantry, by their affections to the clan, and by his power of dispossessing them of their farms. The best of his tenantry were therefore the first to bring forward their sons, when the landlord undertook to raise men for the army. A body of men, so composed, was undoubtedly much superior to a regiment recruited in the ordinary manner; both by the hardihood of the breed, and much more by the feudal feelings of reverence for their officers, pride in their clan, and attachment to each other. But as soon as the feudal state of the country was supplanted by another system, these peculiarities vanished. The low rent of land was the whole foundation upon which they rested. When the chieftain exacts its full value, the relation between him and his tenants is the same as that of a landlord in any other part of the kingdom. The Highland regiments, accordingly, have been approaching, in their composition and character, to a similarity with the other regiments in the service, ever since the advance of rents began to be considerable. We must go back to the Seven-Years' war to find those regiments in their original purity, formed entirely on the feudal principle, and raised in the manner that has been described. Even as early as the American war, some tendency towards a different system was observable; and, during the late war, many regiments were Highland in little else than in name. Some corps were composed nearly in the ancient manner; but there were others, in which few of the men had any connexion whatever with the estates of their officers; being recruited, in the ordinary manner, at Glasgow and other manufacturing places, and consisting of all descriptions of men, Lowlanders and Irish, as well as Highlanders. There is no point, indeed, from which we can see so distinctly the change that has taken place in the whole system of the Highlands, as from this view of the history of the Highland regiments.

II. To such as have formed a correct apprehension of the nature of this essential change, and of the character and circumstances of the tenantry that have been dispossessed of their lands, all projects will appear unavailing to avert their emigration, and all direct restrictions upon it by law, no better than violent injustice. Their removal from the country is a temporary loss, unquestionably, to the public, but one which accompanies the progress of general opulence, the extended establishment of protecting laws, and the consequent amelioration of property and produce. Those who are themselves under no necessity of seeking another home, always look upon emigration itself as the evil that is mixed with these confessed advantages; and they regard it as an evil, only because they imagine that it may have consequences that may possibly somehow or another impair their own perfect security and ease. They do not perceive that the real evil, occasioned by these starts in the general progress, when it suddenly takes a new course, is the disturbance and dispossession of a class of citizens, quite as important and deserving as themselves; quite as desirous, too, of enjoying unimpaired security and ease; but whose habits and attachments are swept away in a sacrifice to the general wealth. Emigration is not the evil, but the remedy; the sad, but single resource of those by whom the real evil is suffered. It can never repair it to them, but inadequately; and it requires such a conquest over the strongest prejudices of the heart, that only the last necessity can inspire sufficient resolution. The family of an hereditary farmer, which for ages has been fastening innumerable roots into the spot on which it grew, may be torn up by force; but when cast out from its native earth, will seek for some other soil that is most nearly congenial. The fate of such will not be indifferent to the statesman; but he will acknowledge that the sufferers must find, in their individual prudence, an alleviation which his rules cannot administer: While he feels for all his people, he will know the limits of his own beneficence; and while he eyes with exultation the spontaneous advancement of opulence and order, will forbear the ineffectual attempt to remove partial evils, or reconcile incompatible advantages.

In the case of the Highland emigrations, some schemes of alleviation have been proposed, out of a feeble and mistaken humanity,—while nothing short of direct restriction would have satisfied, in other persons;—a spirit of injustice which, in its selfishness, was equally mistaken. Agreeably to what often happens in the history of legislation, the only scheme that has been put in practice, was a compromise between the two, and seems to have been imposed by this mistaken self-interest upon that feeble humanity.

The undertaking of great public works in the north, the cultivation of waste lands, the encouragement of the fisheries, and the introduction of manufactures, have been considered by many benevolent and public-spirited persons as appropriate remedies and preventives of emigration. It is sufficient to observe, that not one of them is applicable to the circumstances of those who are inclined to emigrate, and can afford it. The cultivation of waste land, which might appear at first sight rather a promising scheme, only appears so while we forget the soil and climate, and tenures of the Highlands; and the attempts of this kind that have been made by a few proprietors, prove only, that, if conducted on a more judicious plan, it might retain, out of the class of poor cotters, a sufficient number to supply the country fully with day-labourers, but could never be rendered acceptable to tenants even of the lowest order. As to the expectations which have been entertained from the employment afforded by new public works, such as the Caledonian Canal and the Highland roads and bridges, the appropriate utility of those noble undertakings is sufficient praise, without ascribing effects to them for which they are quite inadequate. They may give a temporary relief to some of the peasantry, by bringing employment a little nearer than when it was to be sought in the low country of Scotland: but even the peasant must quit his residence, though not quite so far, to procure this temporary employment: and the tenant, who has been deprived of his land, will still have to ask himself the same question as before, whether he will remove into another part of the country to earn wages as a labourer, or into another country where he may become again a possessor of land. The same remark that has just been made with respect to the cultivation of waste lands, may be extended to the fisheries; they might, if freed from the obstacles by which they are at present discouraged, afford employment to a considerable number of the poorer sort of people. And it is an important reflection, that the general change in the management of the Highland estates, is likely to remove that connexion between fishing and the cultivation of land, which, in the opinion of the most competent judges, has been the greatest impediment to the progress of the fisheries upon the Western coast and Isles. The introduction of manufactures, if it were practicable, would obviously present no object of employment suitable to the displaced tenants. It is unnecessary, therefore, to consider, in this place, the circumstances which appear to render their introduction into the Highlands wholly impracticable.

In all the foregoing schemes it is implied, that the disposition to emigrate arises from unalterable causes, and that it must take its course in the mean while, though we may endeavour to devise measures that shall attract the displaced population into new channels of industry at home. They are dictated, all of them, by genuine motives of patriotism, but have not yet been contrived, nor are ever likely to be contrived in such a form as to render them really applicable to the case. But, upon the subject of the Highland emigrations, we have sometimes been shocked by language which expresses a different spirit, and in a quarter where it is quite as inconsistent and senseless as it is unfeeling. They, however, who have bestowed a slight reflection on the inconsistencies to which men are liable when their interest is involved in a complicated subject, cannot be very much surprised in this instance to find some proprietors, who would willingly profit by the great advance of rents, and at the same time retain the facility of raising a regiment; who like to receive the income of a sheep-farm, to spend in the metropolis, and would still find the splendour of many feudal dependants in the country. These active and most useful depopulators, are sometimes found very indignant declaimers against emigration. From them, but much more from their factors, and from neighbours of an inferior order, who conceive themselves to have an interest in a crowded population, on account of the low wages for which they can then manufacture their kelp, and carry on a few petty branches of traffic, we have sometimes heard such a clamour, as if emigration were a new species of sedition, and it were the duty of the legislature to suppress it by new and absolute restrictions. Our legislature is too well informed to be misled into any injustice so violent and so absurd; and we assuredly despair of convincing those factors that it would be an absurdity and injustice.

Our legislature, however, is not yet so perfectly well informed, as not to have been misled, in consequence of its humanity being imposed upon. During the administration of Mr Addington, an act was passed for regulating the transportation of the emigrants; and the professed object of these regulations was, to enforce a due care of the lives and health of the passengers, and to prevent an undue profit on the part of the owner of the vessel, by crowding it too much. For this purpose, the statute enacts, that no ship shall carry a greater number of persons than in the proportion of one

126

passenger for every two ton; and that every passenger shall be obliged to take $3\frac{1}{2}$ lib. of beef or pork weekly, besides a large allowance of farinaceous food, and that they themselves shall not be at liberty to dispense with any part of this. This attention to the comforts of the emigrants is a little too active: the bill, it is to be observed, went to London from the Highland Society. In the first place, the allowance of room, which is required as absolutely necessary for the health of the passengers, is nearly double that of the transport service; for $1\frac{1}{2}$ ton, allotted for full grown men, is little more than half as much as two tons, allotted for passengers of all ages. The emigrants themselves, in the allowance of birth-room, usually observed a rule, which had been the result of experience, that their whole number, including infants, might be reckoned equivalent to two thirds of that number of grown persons. Surely they might have been left to their own experience in this particular. But, in the second place, the quantity of provisions indispensably forced upon them, is beyond all reasonable proportion; the allowance of farinaceous food alone, exceeds the entire consumption of country labourers in any part of Scotland; and so large an allowance of butcher's meat as $3\frac{1}{2}$ lib. for every passenger, even for infants at the breast, must appear strange to those who know that animal food is so rarely tasted in the Highlands by the lower order of tenantry, that, in the survey published by the Board of Agriculture, it is stated, that, among the farmers, there is not 5 lib. of meat consumed in the family throughout the year. And yet the Highland Society, in their instructions for the framing of this act, recommended 7 lib. a week as absolutely necessary for every passenger. Nobody, after attending to these enactments, will entertain a doubt that their real purpose was to enhance the expense of the voyage, and so render it less within the means of the poor tenants. Such a purpose was not altogether discovered by the Society, and afterwards afforded exultation to many individuals. In the real operation of the act, however, the difference of expense has no other effect but to encroach upon the little stock of cash collected by the emigrants from the sale of their property, and to land them on the foreign shore worse provided for their new exertions. It is superfluous to expose more at large the injustice of such a law. It may easily have been imposed upon the humanity of those who were wholly ignorant of the Highlands and the emigrations. But we cannot so readily acquit them, to whom the circumstances of that country and its dislodged inhabitants were perfectly well known.

III. Since emigration must go on from the Highlands, until the class of small tenants is drained off, it seems desirable that the overflowings of our own population should contribute to the strength and improvement of our own colonies. But, from circumstances, accidental at first, and perpetuated by the natural disposition of the emigrants to follow their relations and friends where almost another home was already formed, most of the emigrations are directed to settlements in the United States. Different districts of the Highlands have different corresponding settlements, to which their emigrants resort. The people in each district have a tolerably accurate knowledge of some particular settlement, where their own connexions have gone; for the Highlanders distrust all information about America that does not come from their own immediate connexions; and in a mountainous country, intelligence seldom spreads far beyond the valley where it is first received. Of every other settlement but their own, the people of each district are usually quite ignorant, or entertain very mistaken notions; and, in particular, those whose views have been directed to the southern States, have received very gloomy impressions of the climate of Canada and the northern colonies.

In Lord Selkirk's apprehension, the importance of securing these emigrants to our own colonies, instead of abandoning them to a foreign country, is rendered more urgent by the peculiar situation of our northern colonies in America. In some of them, it appears, settlers, of by no means a desirable description in respect of character and principles, have intruded themselves, and are fast approaching to a majority of numbers. Nothing would seem more expedient, therefore, for the preservation of these colonies to the mother country, than that a strong barrier should be formed against the contagion of American sentiments, by a body of settlers whose manners and language are distinct, and who inherit ancient feelings of loyalty and military valour.

In order to induce the Highlanders to change the course of their emigrations, determined (as has been already observed) by their gregarious affection, some strong encouragement, in Lord Selkirk's opinion, ought to be held out by Government. The encouragement must be sufficient to induce a considerable body of people, connected by the ties of blood and friendship, to try a new situation; and if such a settlement were once conducted through its first difficulties, till the adventurers felt confidence in their resources, the object might be considered as accomplished. It is not necessary that the inducements should be continued longer than this. But they ought to be of such a nature as to suit those who feel some difficulty, from the narrowness of their means, in executing their design. We perfectly acquiesce in Lord Selkirk's reasoning, that this might be done without increasing the spirit of

128

emigration; or rather that, upon the principles of human nature, it could not be done in such a way as to increase that spirit in the least.

These views presented themselves to Lord Selkirk, upon the eve of the last war. The eventful period that followed, precluded all active prosecution of them; but their importance remained deeply impressed upon his mind, and their practicability was confirmed by all his maturer reflections. On the restoration of peace, the emigrations were recommenced with a spirit more determined and more widely diffused than upon any former occasion. All his views recurred upon him, as demanding immediate attention; and prompted him to represent, to some members of that Administration, the necessity of active interference, in order to attract the emigrants to our own colonies. This representation excited no corresponding interest. Unwilling to abandon the object altogether, Lord Selkirk was led to consider how far it was possible for him, as an individual, to follow it up on a more limited scale, to the effect at least of proving the practicability of the suggestion. Under the assurance of a grant of waste lands belonging to the Crown, upon such terms as promised an adequate return for the unavoidable expenses of the undertaking, he resolved, at his own risk, to try the experiment, and to engage some of the emigrants, who were preparing to go to the United States, to change their destination, and embark for our own colonies. He was given to understand, that it would be more satisfactory to Government, if the people he had engaged were settled in a maritime situation, instead of that which he had at first in contemplation. Though by no means satisfied that this suggestion was founded in just views of national policy, he felt it his duty to acquiesce, and determined on making his settlement in Prince Edward's Island in the Gulph of St Lawrence. To give the experiment a fair prospect of success, he yielded to the necessity of attending the colonists himself.

A description of the settlement, the difficulties that attended it, its progress and final success, forms the last chapter of this work. It does not admit of abridgement; every reader must have thought it too short. The candour with which the first obstacles are described, the practical and profound judgment with which the various means and arrangements appear to have been combined, and that tone of benevolence, without ostentation, and yet thoroughly systematic, which pervades the whole design, renders it the most pleasing and most useful history, that has been given to the world, of the establishment of a new colony. We shall merely enumerate the leading facts. His settlers, to the number of eight hundred persons of all ages, reached Prince Edward's

Island in August 1803; and the spot selected upon this coast for the principal establishment, was almost desert, being separated by an arm of the sea and an interval of several miles from any older settlement. Before the middle of September, the people were dispersed upon their separate lots, and began the cultivation of their farms. The lots were laid out in such a manner, that four or five families built their houses in a little knot together; the distance between the adjacent hamlets seldom exceeding a mile. This social plan of settlement, besides other advantages to recommend it, resembled their style of living in their native country. They were allowed to purchase in fee-simple, and, to a certain extent, on credit: from 50 to 100 acres were allotted to each family at a moderate price, but none was given gratuitously. To accommodate those who had no superfluity of capital, they were not required to pay the price in full till the third or fourth year of their possession; and, in this time, an industrious man may have it in his power to discharge his debt out of the produce of the land. The same principle was adhered to in the distribution of provisions; though several of the poorer settlers could not go on without support, every assistance they received was as a loan, under strict obligations of repayment with interest. They formed their first houses upon the model of those of the American woodsmen. Before the winter set in, they had not only lodged themselves, but made some progress in cutting down the trees; and, upon the opening of the spring, the land was finally prepared for the seed. In September, however, Lord Selkirk quitted the island, leaving the settlement under the charge of a faithful agent, and did not return to it till the end of the same month in the following year. He found the settlers then engaged in securing their harvest; their crop of potatoes alone would have been sufficient for their entire support. Round the different hamlets, the extent of land in cultivation was, at an average, in the proportion of two acres to each able working hand. And several boats had been built, by means of which a considerable supply of fish had been obtained. In the whole settlement he met but two men who showed the least appearance of despondency. The further progress of these colonists is now to be left to their own guidance. Most of them have already proceeded to improve the construction of their houses, less perhaps from a personal desire of better accommodation, than from that pride of landed property which is natural to the human breast, and which, though repressed among the Highland tenantry by recent circumstances, is ready to resume its spring as soon as their situation will permit. Lord Selkirk concludes with observing, that no further doubt can now be entertained of the practicability

130

of inducing the Highlanders to emigrate to our own colonies; and he flatters himself, with great justice, that no immaterial progress has already been made towards this object. In some considerable districts, the current appears already to be decidedly turned; and further exertions of the same kind might secure to our North American possessions all those among our countrymen who cannot be retained in the kingdom. But measures, on so extensive a scale as might be required, can only be accomplished by those to whom the interests of the nation are particularly entrusted.

Such of our readers as have not yet procured the original work, will be much more gratified, we are sure, with the foregoing analysis of its contents, than if we had attempted to throw the general discussions into a form of our own. Nor do we find ourselves provided with any remarks that we can venture to subjoin, either by way of criticism or confirmation. The author has unfolded his reasonings with so much perspicuity, that it would be difficult to lend them additional strength by any further illustrations; and in spite of all our vigilance, we cannot find an exception to any of the general doctrines which he has collaterally interweaved into his argument. There are, indeed, very few specimens of political investigation, more nearly approaching to absolute certainty in its conclusion, than that by which he has deduced the impolicy of attempting, by law, to prevent or to regulate such emigrations as those which have proceeded from the Highlands.

Considering the book in this aspect, it appears to us to possess a permanent value, beyond the effect it is calculated to produce in enlightening our own Government respecting the nature of this actual crisis. Other parts of our empire yet remain to undergo a similar change; and other countries in the world, at least all other countries that are destined to improve, and that include a sufficient extent of territory for the various branches of productive economy. Wherever cultivation may be heightened by the investing of new capital, the minute subdivision of land will be swept away for farmers of a different race; and wherever the extended territory of a thriving nation is diversified by a range of mountains, these will at length be appropriated to pasture walks. The particulars, therefore, which Lord Selkirk has related in the history of the Highlands, may be regarded as the description of a general change; for which, in all such countries, legislators ought to be prepared, that they may not, like our English statesmen of old, even Sir Thomas More and Lord Bacon, mistake, as symptoms of decay and devastation, the movements actually occasioned by the growth of wealth, enterprize, and industry. In this respect, we consider Lord Selkirk as having contributed a new article, very nearly finished in its form, to the general elements of political administration; and as having cast light on one of the most intricate parts of the science of Economy, that in which the theory of wealth and the theory of population are examined in connexion.

Vol. VII ([No. XIV] Jan. 1806), Art. XI (pp. 470–471).
The Wealth of Nations, with Notes, Supplementary Chapters, and a Life of Dr Smith. By William Playfair. London. 1805.

IN the whole course of our literary inquisition, we have not met with an instance so discreditable to the English press, as this edition of the Wealth of Nations. It may be given as a specimen of the most presumptuous book-making. The editor proves himself quite ignorant of his author, and of the science on which that author wrote: he does not scruple, however, sometimes to correct, and sometimes to confirm, what he generally misunderstands in both cases. But what has most moved our indignation, is, that he has presumed to thrust his own supplementary chapters, as he calls them, not in the form of notes or an appendix separate from Mr Smith's text, but into the very body of the work itself, and in the same types; breaking the continuity of the author's great design, and adulterating the purity of its composition with this editor's ignorant and vulgar writing. Our readers must accept of it as a sufficient specimen; that, subjoined to the inimitable digression on the corn laws, and before the reader can proceed to the chapter on treaties of commerce, is a tract of fifteen pages by this Mr Playfair, in which he gives *his* opinion, that monopoly, forestalling, and regrating, exist in the trade of provisions, and that Lord Kenyon had many real and credible proofs of it. We have no objection to this being said by those who have such notions; but it is rather indecent to interpolate them into the text of the Wealth of Nations.

We shall say no more of this publication, except to express our surprise that it should have appeared with the name of so respectable a bookseller; who, having had the original property of this immortal work, might have been expected to feel some tenderness and veneration for its fame. We are happy to announce, that, since the expiration of the original right of property, several editions have been published in different parts of the country; particularly a very cheap one by a bookseller in Newgate street, London, the advertisement of which, addressing this philosophical treatise to artisans and tradesmen, may be regarded as a literary curiosity, and a signal proof of the diffusion of liberal information.

An edition of the Wealth of Nations, with notes by an editor properly qualified, would be a most acceptable publication. It ought to comprise, either in the form of illustrations or of corrections to Mr Smith's propositions, the facts which have been more carefully observed since he turned the attention of men of letters to these subjects, as well as the reasonings which later inquirers have pursued. It would be desirable also, that the editor should be acquainted with those writings which preceded the Wealth of Nations, that he might assign the most important reasonings to their real inventors; and it would be useful to multiply the examples which Mr Smith has taken from the institutions, or statistical experience of foreign countries, to elucidate his general principles: In this respect, considerable assistance might be derived from the French edition of the work by Garnier, and the Spanish edition by Ortiz.